THE GENERATION OF CRYPTO MILLIONAIRES & BILLIONAIRES

THE GENERATION OF CRYPTO MILLIONAIRES & BILLIONAIRES

...HOW THE ADVENT OF BITCOIN & BLOCKCHAIN TECHNOLOGY CHANGED THE WORLD'S GLOBAL FINANCIAL SYSTEM AND LEVELED THE PLAYING FIELD FOR EVERYONE.

BY

LEKE REDDINGTON

Published by Spines
ISBN 979-8-89383-792-6

CONTENTS

DEDICATION

We are a sum-total of what we know, who we know, our upbringing, our environments, our training, our unique gifts, our unique abilities, and where we've traveled to and where we've lived. I dedicate this book first to the Lord Yeshua, my Lord and my Savior, to Whom belongs *all* things, for *by* Him *all* things were created that are in heaven, and on earth, everything that is visible and *invisible*, whether thrones, kingdoms, empires, governments, and powers. *All* things are created *through* Him and *for* Him. And He is before *all* things, and in Him *all* things in the universe are held together in unity, obeying the primeval law of their being.[11]

Secondly, this book is dedicated to the very Person (team) behind the brainchild and invention of Bitcoin and Blockchain Technology, known by his (their) pseudonym name as **Satoshi Nakamoto.** Who conceptualized and developed the open-source, peer-to-peer electronic, digital monetary system on a protocol now called the blockchain technology to create **Bitcoin,** the now world-renowned best-performing asset that has changed and revolutionized the world's global financial system, creating and transferring billions of value across nations, raising many people and countries out of financial mess into abundance, freedom, creativity, productivity and unleashing their geniuses.

Thirdly, this book is dedicated to all my financial mentors, global economy teachers, spiritual fathers, tech leaders, and giants at whose feet I've learned, from whose shoulders I've been privileged to enjoy the awesome benefits of grooming and mentorship, to see better and farther than my contemporaries and generation because I stood on your shoulders.

PREFACE

The World's global financial system has always seemed to be a rigged system with a covert playbook that only a few elites, ultra HNI individuals, wealthy families, institutions, and governments had access to in their favor and advantage, which serves them only and leave the general populace of people all over the world in loss, economic troubles, financial constraints, and lack. Money, Finance, and Economy are things that affect everybody in the world, as our daily living, survival, and activities depend on the world's global financial system.

We lose the money and wealth that we toiled hard and labored diligently for to inflation, national currency devaluation, economic depression, recession, geopolitical wars, global economic crisis, corruption, governments misappropriations of funds, wrong economic policies and regulations set by our political leaders and policy makers that keeps us working and working even into our retirement age, with barely little or nothing to hold on to with value.

But now, this narrative and dynamic is changing with the innovation and creation of Bitcoin and Blockchain technology, ideas which were born out of the global economic and financial crisis that happened in 2008-2009, which left many people losing their money, wealth, and assets to economic forces with powers beyond their control. The advent of Bitcoin and Blockchain technology over the last decade is now changing the world's global financial system and leveling the playing field for everyone to take advantage of it for their financial freedom while also hedging their money, wealth, and assets against all national and global economic forces that they cannot fight against or beat.

Many individuals are now setting the pace and blazing the trails for others to follow as they champion the cause for financial freedom, financial independence, productivity, economic growth, and national development in their various fields, especially in the Blockchain industry. We are privileged and greatly blessed to have been born at a time such as this, where we can determine our own financial future by ourselves and make a lasting, valuable impact in the lives of our family, friends, community, society, countries, and the world at large. Many a generation would have loved to have this great opportunity and advantage that we have access to now with Bitcoin and Blockchain Technology which they did not have access to in their own days and time.

CHAPTER 1

HISTORY OF MONEY AND FINANCE

What do you really think Money is? I know you would probably think it's the physical paper currency notes that you are holding in your hands or that you have and see in your pocket wallet, the dollars, yen, pounds, euros, rands, naira, cedis, or any known currency denomination of the whatever nation or country that you live in, work in, and carry out your businesses. Well, don't be too shocked or surprised if I tell you that all of these that you have thought to be Money, are not Money.

What you thought was Money, the physical paper fiat currency that you know, see, hold, and touch, is just a means of representation of value transfer that also serves as a medium of exchange for quality goods, services, products, and value rendered by any individual, institution, or governments. The real, genuine, and authentic Money cannot be seen with your physical, optical eyes because it's seen in thoughts, ideas, value addition, inventions, problem-solving, and mental mind that births growth, productivity, and abundance.

BARTERING

You grew up to see the known paper money (fiat currency) as money, but long before you were born, as far back as 5,000 years ago, Money was in existence, and yet it did not exist in the form of a paper fiat currency that you know today[2]. Money existed in various forms, such as cattle, farm produce (yam tubers, wheat, cotton, grains, etc.), gold, silver, precious stones, gems, seashells, precious oil, etc., which can be traded or bartered as a mean of exchange and used as a store of value and wealth.

This Bartering process involves a direct trade of goods and services. For instance, a farmer may exchange a bag of wheat for a pair of shoes from a shoemaker. However, this Bartering process takes time, especially if it involves services rendered. For instance, if you exchange an axe as part of a Bartering process in which the other party is supposed to kill a woolly mammoth, you have to find someone who thinks the tool (axe) is a fair trade for having to face down the 12-foot tusks of a mammoth. If it doesn't work, you would have to alter the deal until you find someone who will agree to the terms of the Bartering process.

With Time, a type of currency slowly developed over the centuries that involves easily traded items like animal skins, furs, precious stones, salt, and weapons. These traded goods serve as the medium of exchange (Money) even though the value of each of these items was still negotiable in many cases. This Bartering process of trading as a medium of exchange spread across the world and still survives today in some parts of the globe.

THE INVENTION OF MEASURED OR QUANTIFIED MONEY

One of the greatest achievements of the invention of Measured or Quantified Money (Metal Coinage) was the increased speed at which business, services, and value addition could be done very fast, whether it be cutting down huge timbers, mammoth slaying, building a temple, a palace or hiring mercenaries.

According to History, in August 2021, a group of Chinese archaeologists with the State University of Zhengzhou discovered the world's oldest known, securely dated coin minting site in Guanzhuang in Henan Province, China. A mint is a facility where currency (Measured or Quantified Money) is created or minted. Sometime around 640 BCE, this facility began striking spade coins, one of the first standardized forms of metal coinage.[3]

Also, during this same period, further west in the sixth century BCE, Greek poet Xenophanes, quoted by the historian Herodotus, ascribed the invention of metal coinage to the Lydians. In 600 BCE, Lydia's King Alyattes minted what is believed to be the first official currency (Measured or Quantified Money), the Lydian stater. The coins were made from electrum, a mixture of silver and gold that occurs naturally, and the coins were stamped with pictures that acted as denominations. In the streets of Sardis, in approximately 600 BCE, a clay jar might cost you two owls and a snake. Lydia's currency helped the country increase both its internal and external trading systems, making it one of the richest empires in Asia Minor. Today, when someone says, "as rich as Croesus," they are referring to the last Lydian King who minted the first gold coin.[4]

THE PAPER CURRENCY

With Time comes growth and development of new, better means of exchange called the Paper currency. In 1260 CE, the

Yuan dynasty of China moved from coins to paper money.[5] By the time Marco Polo, a Venetian merchant, explorer, and writer who traveled through Asia along the Silk Road, visited China in approximately 1271 CE, the emperor of China had a good handle on both the Money supply and its various denominations. In fact, in the place where modern American bills say, "In God We Trust," the Chinese inscription at the time warned: Those Who are counterfeiting will be beheaded."

Although some parts of Europe still used metal coins as their sole form of currency until the 16th century. The Colonial acquisitions of new territories via European conquest provided new sources of precious metals and enabled European nations to keep minting a greater quantity of coins. Banks that act as stores or treasury houses for this Money (coins) started using paper banknotes for depositors (those who bring their coins, measured and quantified money) and borrowers (those who collect money for personal and business use) to carry around in place of metal coins due to the heavyweight, theft, convenience, and risk associated with carrying plenty of heavy coins around on a long journey or business trips.

These Banknotes could be taken to the Bank at any time and exchanged for their face value in metal, usually silver or gold coins. This Paper Money could be used to buy goods and services. In this way, it operated much like today's Paper Currency (fiat) does in our modern fast world, but unlike today, the Paper Currency during these times was backed by their equivalent silver or gold coins in the Bank's Treasury. During these times, the Paper banknotes were also issued strictly and directly by the Banks and Private financial institutions and not by the Governments of Countries as we have it today.[6]

Also, today, our Paper Currency (fiat) is not backed by their real equivalent of what they are worth in terms of measured or quantified money, the silver or gold coins rather, they are backed by a promise (trust in the Government that issues them) and enormous debt and credit systems which is one of the major reasons why the world's global economy and financial is experiencing a crisis and turmoil. We will talk more about this in future chapters as we journey together across the pages of this book.

The first Paper Currency issued by European governments was issued by their colonial governments in North America; because shipments between Europe and the colonies in North America took a long time, colonies ran out of cash. Instead of going back to the Barter system, the colonial governments issued IOUs that traded as currency. The first instance was in Canada (then a fresh colony) in 1685, when soldiers were issued playing cards denominated and signed by the governor to use as cash instead of coins from France. Amazing and funny, right? I am sure you are getting the idea of what forms or creates Money in our minds. Money is primarily a function of Trust, Recognition, Credibility, and general Acceptance of whatever form it is represented in, as a means of store of value and exchange.

The Paper Currency, with time, moved from being backed by an equivalent value in precious metals, silver, and gold coins to being backed by nothing other than a Promise, Trust, Debt, and Credit by the Governments of the countries that are issuing them. This is what we call The Fiat Paper currency in the world today, which was triggered when the then known President of the United States of America, President Richard Nixon, in 1971 removed the US Dollars from being backed by Gold; this is known as the Gold Standard.

President Nixon suspended the convertibility of the US Dollar to Gold. This Fiat Paper currency has no intrinsic value and has no use value; it is only useful because a lot of people all over the world believe in it and agree that it is a medium of exchange, that it will be accepted by merchants, businesses, corporations for conducting business and value transfer. This is majorly because the Governments of these countries all over the world issue these Fiat Currencies, whether it be US Dollars, Yen, Euros, Pounds, Rands, or Naira etc., are issued as legal tender globally. The word Fiat is derived from the Latin word "fiat," meaning "Let it be done," used in the sense of an order, decree, or resolution.

MOBILE MONEY PAYMENTS

The 21st century gave rise to a novel form of payment activated with the touch of your finger. Mobile Money Payments refer to money used to pay for goods and services. They can also be used to transfer Money (Value) to another individual, such as a family member or friend. This can all be done using a portable electronic device, such as a smartphone or tablet device. This form of payment first came to prominence in Asia and Europe before moving over to North America. From payments via text message, the technology evolved to allow cheques to be deposited using the camera app on smart devices.

Mobile payment services like Apple Pay, Google Pay, and Opay are vying for retailers to accept their platforms for point-of-sale payments. There are also apps dedicated to this method of payment, including Venmo, PayPal, Mastercard, etc.

DIGITAL CURRENCY

With the advent of Technology, Digital Currencies have now been created as the new forms of Money that are backed by emerging Blockchain Technology, Mathematics, Computer Science, Cryptography, and Protocols. Digital Currencies are only available in electronic form, and they cannot be seen with physical eyes or touched or kept in physical bags. Digital Currencies are stored and traded using computer applications or specially designed software. The appeal of virtual Digital

Currencies is that they offer transparency, security, faceless, trustless, no third-party interference, faster, easy, convenient, and the promise of lower transaction fees than traditional online payment mechanisms do and are operated by decentralized authorities and protocols unlike government-issued currencies.

Bitcoin is the standard and pioneering Digital Currency that was created in the year 2009 by Satoshi Nakamoto. It records every transaction carried out on the blockchain ledger with verifiable open source across several validators who validate the transactions on the Blockchain. Transactions cannot be manipulated, duplicated, reversed, or faked because it operates on a public ledger that is accessible and transparent for all to scrutinize and verify. As of today, 31st of August 2023, the value and worth of Bitcoin in circulation is about $530 Billion US dollars[7], with a total max supply of 21 million, and a unit piece of Bitcoin is valued at about $27,000. This is remarkable, considering this is during a global bear market period as compared to during the bull market in 2021, when Bitcoin was at its all-time high of $69,000 per unit. It's worthy of note to point out that this same Bitcoin was trading for less than a single dollar $1 when it was created a decade ago; it was valued at $0.39 for a unit piece in 2010.[8]

Although Bitcoin is the most popular and first Digital Currency, there are other Digital Currencies that have been developed on quicker, faster, more transactions, larger blockchain technology like Ethereum, Ripple (XRP), Binance (BNB), Dogecoin, WikiCat (WKC), Solana (SOL), etc The Digital Currencies world also knowns as Cryptocurrencies has over 22,000+ digital currencies with various technology, layers, protocols, themes and solutions they are trying to solve.[10]

They are often referred to as Altcoins, and there are some Digital Currencies, also called Stable coins, pegged to another asset's price to correlate to a value of $1. They serve as the bridge or meeting point of fiat currency and digital currency for easy conversion. Some examples; are USDT, USDC. Also, some Digital Currencies are called Meme coins, like Shina Inu, Dogecoin, etc. They are often for fun, entertainment, and for easy education purposes of the Digital currency. Cryptocurrencies represent an important technological, financial, economic, and computer science innovation, they are considered to be risky because it's a new emerging technology that is just gaining adoption and because of no regulation and governmental or institutional controls around it.[11]

FROM HISTORY TO THE FUTURE

The History of Money is still being written. The system of exchange has moved from swapping animal skins to minting coins to printing paper money, and today, we appear to be on the cusp of a massive shift to electronic digital transactions. Ancient transaction forms have been co-opted: for example, Bartering still occurs on the margins of some markets, such as the business-to-business (B2B) space and some consumer services. The World's global financial and monetary system will surely continue to evolve and change rapidly as humans develop better, improved technologies that provide solutions and make things easier and faster for them for their daily lives and business engagements.

CHAPTER 2
THE ENGINE THAT CONTROLS THE ECONOMY OF NATIONS

One thing that affects everyone in the world today is the Economy; it doesn't matter your level of education, your pedigree, your level of influence or affluence, your networks and relationships, whether you are rich or poor, whether you are great or small. You will always be affected and concerned by the Economy of the Nation, where you live, where you were raised, where you migrated to, and where you conduct your businesses. Amazingly, the world is now a global village. The ripple effect of one Nation far away in Asia (China) can affect the economy of another nation in Africa (Nigeria) or another country is North America (USA).

The Economy of Nations is now so interwoven, intertwined, complex, and interdependent that Government officials, parastatals, and leaders now need to pay attention to understand how the Economy of their Nations functions and work, in relation to their neighboring nations, their Geopolitical economy, their continental economy and the global economy, that gives them the bigger picture of the entire landscape and vision of how to navigate their people and nation out of economic meltdown, economic depression, economic recession, large fiscal debts to other countries, management of their foreign reserves, handling of their international trade settlement systems and policies that governs their trade with other nations. Without the proper understanding of this, it has been hard and difficult for the Leaders of these nations to steer their people and country in the right direction towards their development, growth, productivity, and advancement of their citizens and nation and to be a worthy, recognized, honorable and delightsome nation on a global scale.

It's shocking and unraveling to note that many of the world's government leaders and policy makers have little or no understanding of how the engine that controls the economy of their nation works. We vote into power presidents, politicians, policy makers, public analysts, and strategists that have no sound management of their own personal economy and finance. How can the blind lead the blind? Yet, they sit at the top affairs of Nations to make decisions and policies that lead to economic crash that drives inflation to alarming rates as high as double digits (Turkey 73%, Argentina 72.4%, Nigeria 24%),[12] some as crazy to triple digits (Zimbabwe 289%, Venezuela 210%),[13] high number of unemployment, low GDP, low foreign investors drive, slow economic growth rate, high insecurity and many other economic vices.

It's of utmost importance to have the right people running the affairs of the Economy of their nations, to stir the countries affairs in the right direction for economic growth and development. When this is rightly done, nations and governments will not be putting square pegs in round holes to manage the affairs of the economy of their nations. It's important to note that selecting a round peg for a round hole is not by the number of universities they've attended, the number of university degrees they have, their Masters, MBA, PhD in Economics, or whatever. Education is very important to the makeup of an individual's life and society development, but understanding how the engine of the Economy of the Nations works is not primarily a function of universities, certifications, and occupation, but rather having the insight, wisdom, light, vision, ingenuity, courage, heart, love, selflessness, knowledge and understanding of the Economy on a personal scale, community scale, regional scale, national scale, continental scale, and then on a global scale.

UNDERSTANDING ECONOMY

Have you ever been asked what is Economy? You don't have to be confused and troubled by all the terminologies, theories, definitions, and complexities on Economy. The great Albert Einstein is often quoted to have said that, "If you can't explain it to a six-year-old, then you don't really understand it." As we journey together along the pages of this book, I will strive to ensure that you gain the understanding and knowledge of how the Engine that controls the Economy works like a six-year-old child. I'll ensure that you gain the picture and clarity in simple and well-defined terms for easy comprehension and understanding. Like one of my financial mentors, Robert Kiyosaki will say, "Economy and Finance is not rocket science; you just need an open mind that is willing to learn the fundamentals."

What is Economy? Economy is simply the process within a domain (personal or general) that looks into the production, distribution, and consumption of goods and services and the supply of money in that domain (which can be personal or general countries, regions, or global). Without a viable, strong Economy, the domain (personal or general) will collapse because it deals directly with wealth, welfare, humans need, wants, scarcity, resources, individual and national productivity, management of money, financial dynamism, growth, development and advancement of the domain (personal or general). This is one of the reasons why the economy affects everybody, no matter how strata and placement in life, because we are all humans.

The intertwined, multiple interdependence of us humans on each other is what makes Economics (a subject focused on Economy) to be a science or field that has stakes or interests in many other fields like political science, geography, mathematics, sociology, psychology, engineering, law, medicine, business, craftmanship, sales and marketing. This is because one must be well grounded and holistic in their approach and understanding of Economy from its multifaceted areas as we humans are diverse.

The central quest of sound economics is to determine the most logical and effective use of resources to meet personal and national goals. Production and employment, investment and savings, health, money, and banking system, government policies on taxation and spending, international trade, industrial organization and regulation, urbanization, environmental issues, and legal matters such as the design and enforcement of property rights, are just a little of the concerns at the heart of the science of economics.

PERSONAL ECONOMY, NATIONAL ECONOMY, AND GLOBAL ECONOMY

As explained earlier, that Economy is a function of a domain system; the domain can be within your personal individual life, or within the domain of the country where you are resident, or within the domain of the world at large that you live in as a human. This means that when it comes to Economy, you can either zoom in or zoom out of each domain to have a better picture, perspective, and understanding of what is happening within each of these domains and how each affects you. How it affects your welfare, how it affects your comfort, your freedom, your community, your kids and your family, your community, your country and how it affects the world at large.

When you take focus on your personal economy as it relates to your personal individual human actions and decisions. How you analyze, manage, and use your personal resources (scarce, limited, or unlimited), like your time, money, skills, food, labor, land, etc., to achieve the most satisfactory and fulfilling allocation of your resources to solve your personal problems and challenges in order to live the best possible life available for you. The daily and life-long decisions that you make based on this towards your personal economy are often referred to as Microeconomics. Examples of common day-to-day economic questions you will be faced with are: should I borrow a loan? Should I get a mortgage? Should I pay cash or use my credit card? Should I open a 401K plan or mutual fund account? Should I open a Bitcoin wallet account? Wise Economists understand how to make these decisions in their own lives and can give sound advice to others on a personal and professional level.

When you zoom out of your personal economy to look into your countries or neighboring nations and the world at large as it relates to the dynamism that controls how your country works and the world works, paying attention to the inflation levels, price levels, rate of growth, GDP (Gross Domestic Product), national income, unemployment rates, consumer price index, foreign investors growth, foreign exchange rate, import and export trade policies. Now, you are delving into the national and global economy, which is often referred to as macroeconomics. Your mind will begin to ask questions like: Why is a nation as rich with mineral resources like my country in so much debt to another foreign nation? Why are my country's citizens not receiving the best welfare and care possible despite all our technological advancements? Who determines how much money is circulating in my country? Why are there so many unemployed people in my nation? Why has our inflation rate been rising consecutively for months?

From World Leaders to Presidents to Politicians to Educators to journalists to Urban Planners, a thorough understanding of Macroeconomics has a strong impact on leadership skills, decision-making, and the ability to plan for a flourishing, wealthy, prosperous, and vibrant social future.

THE ENGINE THAT DRIVES THE ECONOMY OF NATIONS

The principles and theories that back the operations and dynamism of the world's economy can be complex and sometimes hard to understand, but like I said earlier, one of the main aims of this book is to break them down for your easy understanding like for a six-year-old talked about by Albert Einstein. I am a proud, longtime, astute student of one of the world's greatest economists and hedge fund manager, Ray Dalio of Bridgewater Associates, the one-time CEO and founder of the world's largest asset management company with assets under management of about $150 Billion US Dollars.[14]

I love Ray Dalio so much for a lot of reasons, and he is one of my biggest inspirations in the world of finance and economy. One of the many reasons why I love Ray Dalio is his uncanny ability and wittiness to explain tough, hard, technical, economic concepts and theories in simple, easy to understand terms for his students. For me, He is like the man called Daniel, also known as Belteshazar in scripture, who had an excellent spirit, light, and understanding, with the ability to explain hard theories and dissolve doubts.[15] My first comprehensive understanding of how the Engine that controls the economy works was learned from Ray Dalio, but now I've modified the concept for a better understanding for people, especially in the developing nations in Africa and Asia.

THE ECONOMY MACHINE

The Machine that controls or drives the world's economy is simple, but a lot of people in the world don't understand it or have an idea of what it is, yet they are involved and participate in the Economic Machine daily through their actions, inactions, decisions, policies, etc. While the Economy of a Nation may look very big and complex, at its most basic cell unit, it is just underpinned by simple transactions that are driven by human nature of having their daily needs met, repeated a zillion of times across various sectors (health, food, agriculture, oil, communication, construction, transportation, technology, entertainment, etc.), all across the nation, regional countries, and the entire globe.

Transactions are the basic cell unit of every Economy. Transactions are essentially the exchange of money or credit between a buyer and seller for goods and services rendered or for financial assets that increase in value or produce income over time. This is how individuals, businesses, banks, and Government all operate to have the money or income needed to cater to their personal and national needs and welfare. Price is the amount or result of **total spending/quantity sold**. Transactions are the building blocks and most important unit of the Economic Machine. If you understand how Transactions work, you will understand the whole economy. The Economy is the sum of all transactions in it, which can run into billions, trillions, and zillions over time. Money and Credit account for the total spending in an economy, and they are key drivers.

THE MARKET, GOVERNMENT AND CENTRAL BANK

All Buyers and Sellers making Transactions represent the Market. For instance, we have stock markets, oil markets, wheat markets, crypto markets, and so on. The combination of all of these sub-markets is the entire Market or the entire Economy. Governments are the biggest Buyers and Sellers in markets. Another major player in the Economy of a nation is the Central Bank of the country, such as the Federal Reserve in the United States, which controls the amount of Money and Credit in the Economy, which it does by regulating or influencing the interest rates and the printing of money.

The Central Bank of any nation is fundamental in the control of the Economy because the Central Bank controls the Flow of Credit. You may want to ask, what is Credit? Credit is simply the ability of a Buyer to obtain goods and services without making Money payment for it, based on the Trust that the Money will be paid in the future, based on the time and agreement made between the Buyer and the Seller. Credit is the most important part of the economy because it is the biggest and most volatile part.

As a result of the existence of Credit, there will surely be Debtors and Creditors, Lenders and Borrowers. Lenders (Individuals, Banks, Governments, etc.) lend money to make more of it, expecting that the Borrowers will use it to create goods and services, purchase assets, and for value creation that helps them to generate more income or money. On the other hand, Borrowers borrow money to buy something they can't afford, such as a house, a car, a business, or stocks. Borrowers promise to repay the amount borrowed (principal) with interest. When Interest rates are high, the borrowing will be low because of the additional repayment on the Credit or Loan. When interest rates are low, borrowing is high, people take on more debt and use more credit to make purchases of goods and services provided in the Markets of the Economy. All these factors and parameters put together drive the Machine of the Economy for growth, productivity, and job creation.

Credit created out of thin air by many Banks and Governments is the major driver of a lot of National economies in the world today, with a ripple effect of each country affecting one another during a global economic depression or recession. For example, the economy of the United States of America is based on Credit, like most countries in the world, backed by the promissory fiat currency issued by the Governments. Out of the entire Money in circulation in the US, 95% of it is based on Credit, and 5% is based on physical Money (fiat dollar). And yet, the U.S. economy accounts for 25.4% of the world's global economy.[16] The U.S current debt deficit is at a whopping $31 Trillion dollars as of May 2023.[17]

Credit is important to most countries participating in the world's global economy because it means Borrowers can increase their Spending. This is very vital in driving the nation's economy because one person's or nation's spending is another person's or nation's income. This means that the other person, on the back of an increase in income and more credit trustworthiness by Lenders, that they will repay their principal with interest can now borrow more money to increase their own spending, which in turn becomes someone else's income. This creates a cycle, per the chart below.

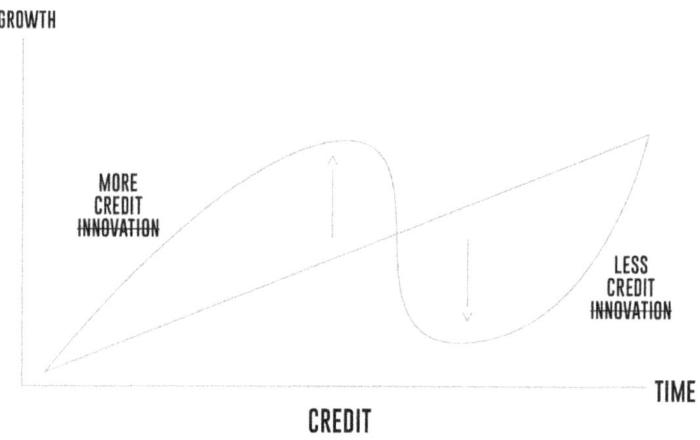

The 3 Forces that drive the Economy Machine

1. Productivity
2. Short-term Debt Cycle
3. Long-term Debt Cycle

PRODUCTIVITY GROWTH

Over time, as we grow up into adulthood, we go to school, we learn a skill or craft, we accumulate knowledge, we create things, we invent and innovate, we produce food, basic needs, and necessities of life for our welfare and comfort. All of this drives the productivity growth of our individual lives and our personal economy. The multiplied effect of this across our community, state, and country drives the productivity growth and national economy of our countries. The Productivity Growth doesn't fluctuate much, so it's not a big driver of economic swings, but Debt is a major driver.

DEBT

Debt is a financial obligation that one entity owes to another. Individuals, businesses, and governments take on debt in order to support themselves, make purchases, or invest in their future growth. Individual consumer Debt is seen in things like Credit Cards, Loans, Vehicle Financing, and Mortgages. Corporations often also take out debt in the form of lines of credit and corporate loans, among others. Debt allows us to consume more than we produce when it is acquired, and it forces us to consume less when we have to pay it back.

There are two types of Debt Cycles: Short-term Debt Cycle and Long-term Debt Cycle. These Debt Cycles cause a swing that is called a "Debt Swing." The short term happens within every 5 to 8 years, and the long term happens within 75 to 100 years. These Debt Cycles are often not noticed because we are all living in our day-to-day activities, all about our various jobs and businesses. Days run into weeks, weeks run into months, months runs into years, years run into decades, and we are all oblivious and naïve of what's happening in our national and global economy and how both are affecting our personal economy, our personal lives, welfare, comfort, productivity, income, and freedom. In the same way, we really don't notice the day-to-day changes happening in our physical bodies as we grow older, based on the choices of food or diet we are taking, our decision on choosing healthy meals, exercising, and living healthy. Until we look at ourselves in the mirror one day, and then boom, we have a health crisis or a bad doctor's report that calls our attention to it or how fast and suddenly we've aged due to stress.

Without Credit or Debt in the Economy, the only way to improve and grow it is by working harder and smarter, bringing more value addition and creation to the economy table. This approach is slow and linear, as represented by the diagonal line in the chart below.

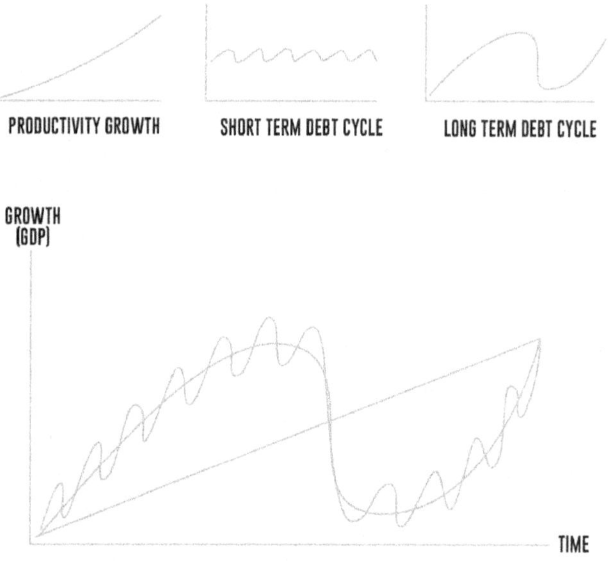

DEBT CYCLES

Every time you or your country borrow, you and your country are effectively borrowing Money from your Future self because the borrowed Money called Loan that has become a Credit will need to be paid back by you and your country later in the future. Your future self will need to spend less than they make or must produce more and generate more income in order to pay the Debt owed from the Credit. And if you and your country choose to default in the payment of the fund, which leads to more problems because you and your country have literally stolen money from the individual or country that the money was borrowed from. This is one of the key drivers behind the economic collapse of nations and global economic crisis when there are major defaults in payments of credit and debts owed.

These series of default and debt management crises set into action a mechanical, predictable sequence of events that affects everyone, from the haves to the have-nots, from the rich to the poor, from the great to the small. Credit isn't necessarily bad. It's like a tool or a gun; it's how it's been handled or managed that determines if its outcome or consequence will be bad or good. It becomes a menace when it finances over consumption and accumulation of liabilities, corruption, and misappropriation of the funds, making the funds difficult to be paid back like Greece, Portugal, Italy, and Spain during the 2010s, and in many African countries like Nigeria, Zimbabwe, and Asia countries.

In our personal individual lives, it's important that we understand how to handle our debts and credit system. Buying a consumable like a television or a car without using it to generate income via e-transport like Uber, Bolt is a bad debt. Whereas buying a vending machine or a tractor for agricultural produce will generate income to pay back the debt and enjoy a better-quality life is a good debt. Debt is also called Other People's Money by one of my financial mentors, Robert Kiyosaki, the author of the world's bestselling personal finance book "Rich Dad, Poor Dad." Debt, when used well and efficiently, it helps to create wealth and freedom. We will talk more about this in Chapter 9: Financial Education, Intelligence, and Freedom.

Every Debt Cycle that goes up must eventually later come now, whether for short-term or long-term cycles.

SHORT-TERM DEBT CYCLE

The first phase of the cycle is called Expansion because Spending increases in the economy, which increases Incomes and asset value also increases alongside the cost of goods and services, which also increases, and this leads to inflation. When spending increases faster than the production of goods, it means that we have more demand than supply, which results in inflation. The Central Bank of each country in the world manages the Inflation by raising interest rates, which makes Credit more expensive and decreases the Borrowing, Spending, and Incomes in the country. This results in what is called Deflation – Prices of assets, goods, and services coming back down. The bobbling economic activity decreases, and if this goes unchecked this can lead to a Recession.

At this point, the Central Banks decrease interest rates in order to stimulate borrowing and spending, boost economic activity, and get the economy out of recession. When Credit is readily made available in the economy, this leads to economic expansion; when it is not, it leads to recession. This short-term debt cycle lasts for about 5 to 8 years and happens over and over again for decades. The peak and trough of the cycle end up higher and higher with each subsequent cycle which means more growth and more Debt is accumulated. This accumulated Debt for decades leads us to the long-term debt cycle.

LONG-TERM DEBT CYCLE

The Long-term Debt cycle is the cumulative of the short-term debt cycle for over a period of 75 years to 100 years. Despite the high Debt deficit and defaults by most individuals, corporations, banks, financial houses, and governments that were accumulated during the short-term debt cycles, Lenders still keep on lending money because the world's financial system is highly dependent on Debt and Credit systems. The perspective and paradigm of the modern-day world is so fixed on quick fixes, short-term solutions, long-throating, and keeping up with their next-door neighbors that it leads to high incomes, soaring asset prices, booming stock markets, and so on.

Oftentimes, it only takes a temporal or major setback like COVID-19, the Geopolitical war between Russia and Ukraine, the unprecedented rise of inflation (high cost of goods), and unemployment for us to realize the poor choices and decisions we've been making with our finances as individuals, as well as a nation over the years, decades and century that is now boomeranging on us. This consequence of our poor choices and decisions with respect to our nation's economy and finance is what we call Economic Bubble.

THE DEBT BURDEN

The Financial burden in our personal individual lives and as a nation is often a factor of the level of Debt and Credit that we owe as individuals, as well as a nation in direct relation to our level of value creation, productivity, income generation, products, and services that we offer, as individuals and as a Nation.

When the balance of our income generation, productivity, and value creation is almost the same or greater than our debt and credit that we owe, as seen in the image above, we have a good or effective debt burden. We won't be under undue pressures, stress, and economic challenges that arise as a result of bad Debt burden.

However, when our nation or individual Debt growth surpasses our nation or personal Income Growth/Productivity and Value Creation. This Debt Growth to Income Growth ratio is the Debt Burden. People might feel wealthy as the value of their seeming assets increases because when they go to their Banks and Lenders, they measure their wealth by the material things that they possess, like cars and houses on mortgage, which are used as collaterals that underpin their borrowings, without really realizing that these things are more of liabilities than assets because they take money from them, depreciate in value over time and they do not bring in money or increase in value over time.

Like a wise philosopher once said, we shouldn't conflate the trappings of success with success itself. The more people take on debt and pay it back as their income rises in relation to this, they become more creditworthy to borrow more and spend more and feel wealthy when they use these funds to finance their excesses, exuberance, and liabilities instead of deploying the borrowed money to wise, frugal, creative use and value creation that creates goods and services, that generate more income or revenue for them. This is also the same for our governments and nations when they misappropriate funds that they receive from other global financial institutions like IMF, EU, UN, WHO and from other stronger economic nations.

As the Debt Burden increases, the value of these collaterals can vanish and depreciate very fast, and as the Debt burden increases, it creates larger debt repayments over decades, eventually hitting a peak like during the economic crash of the global financial crisis in 2008, with Japan in 1989, and during the great depression in 1929. At this point, spending goes backwards, borrowing stalls, incomes drop, asset values plummet, stock markets tank, and social tensions rise – this is called Deleveraging. It's little compared to what we are seeing today; the ripple effect of the COVID-19 crisis isn't a result of a long-term debt cycle but through a force majeure external event and Government interventions to prevent the economy from crumbling and giving support to many people for their welfare.

When the value of the collateral that was used as a means of security for the loans is gone, and Banks find themselves in trouble. This often leads to the massive bailouts of the so called "too big to fail" Banks that control the economy of nations, like JP Morgan, Goldman Sachs, Wells Fargo, State Street, and others in a massive $700 Billion bailout bill called Emergency Economic Stabilization Act in 2008 signed by President George W. Bush[18]. The Lehman Brothers weren't so lucky; with their Bank's stocks plummeting up to 93% during the economic crash, they had to file for bankruptcy with over $619 Billion dollars in Debts of customers, businesses, institutions, and government parastatals money. It was the largest corporate bankruptcy filing in the history of the United States of America.[20] This happened in 2008, barely 15 years ago, and with what we can see coming ahead from our fundamental and technical economic analysis, another greater global economic crash is already looming on the rise. It's a matter of when it will happen, not if it will happen.

During this period of Economic Deleveraging in the Long-term Debt cycle, interest rates can no longer be used to stimulate the economy because they are already at almost zero. The key difference between a recession and a deleveraging is that the Debt Burden is too big and can't be relieved or controlled any longer by lowering the interest rates. When the economic situation gets to this stage, how do we solve it? This moves us to the 4 levers used in Deleveraging the Economy.

FOUR LEVERS FOR DELEVERAGING THE ECONOMY

During an Economic crash or global financial crisis, there are four levers that we can use to deleverage the Economy.

Lever 1: Cut Spending

It's important to cut personal, business, and government spending to be able to pull out of the financial and economic mess caused by the large Debt burden that has accumulated over time for long decades. Strong essential austerity measures are to be put in place by individuals, businesses, and governments of nations. Although, this lever will cause incomes to fall because remember, one person's spending is another person's income, so the debt burden gets even bigger because people can't afford to repay their debts anymore.

The Lever of Cutting Spending is deflationary and painful; the effect of this will be felt in the nation, government, business, and personal individuals' life. As businesses, banks, corporations, and governments begin to cut costs further, this will mean fewer jobs and higher unemployment.

Lever 2: Reduce Debt

Individual, Business, and Government Debts can be reduced through defaults and restructuring. When Banks are squeezed, and businesses can't repay their loan, with individuals lining up to withdraw their money from the Banks for fear of it not being there tomorrow in case of a Bank default or declaring Bankruptcy, you are likely looking at a Depression.

Debt Default
This happens when there is a failure in repayment of the loans. This immediately and directly impacts the defaulting of the Government's bondholders and has dire downstream consequences for the entire economy and people of a nation, which is why countries like Greece were bailed out by the deeper-pocketed EU compatriots, even though the likes of countries like Germany ultimately benefitted.[20]

Debt Restructuring
This happens when Lenders get paid back less or are paid back over a longer period of time or at a more reduced interest rate. Lenders, Banks, and Governments that give out borrowed funds or credit would rather have a little of something than all of nothing, and ultimately this helps to reduce Debt.

However, Debt Restructuring also causes income and asset values to disappear faster, again causing the Debt Burden to get worse. Tackling a Nation's debt challenges and problems is not often as easy as it is, when the borrowed funds were being received. This Debt reduction lever is also painful and deflationary as well. The Government of the nation is impacted because it is now collecting fewer taxes because unemployment has risen, and yet needs to spend more. They need to create stimulus plans to increase spending in the economy. Central Banks are also affected because they now get fewer fees and interest charges, less money and yet the Central Bank needs to lend more funds out to the people and economy.

With all these going on, the Government's budget deficit explodes because it now needs to spend more than it earns in taxes and income revenue as a nation. In order to fund this deficit, it either needs to raise taxes, borrow more money, or do both. And with the unemployment at a high rate, where do those taxes come from? Of course, the seemingly Rich (high-income earners and professionals in the E and S Quadrants), but not the Wealthy (the venture capitalists, investors, and big business owners).

Lever 3: Redistribute Wealth from Haves to Have-Nots

This can be a very dramatic and drastic measure, like Robin Hood stealing from the rich to give to the poor, and incomes are redistributed. This can result in the wealthy being squeezed and resenting the have-nots, and vice versa for the contrast in outcomes. If this continues and it's sponsored or enforced by the Governments, this can lead to social disorder, and revolution can follow, both within and outside the countries, as was the case in the 1930s when Adolf Hitler came to power due to economic collapse in Germany during the great depression in 1929.[21] The pressure to end the depression mounts, but with no Credit system in the market, and with most "money" being credit as explained earlier, the only option left for the Governments and Central Banks is the lever 4.

Lever 4: The Printing of Money

When the interest rates are already at almost zero, the Government of the country and Central Bank are forced to print more money to stimulate the economy. This is inflationary and stimulative, although it can decrease the value of a currency, especially if too much has been printed over time. For instance, the US Dollar has lost over 95% of its value and purchasing power since 1971,[22,] when it was removed from the gold standard, which has allowed the Government to print tons of billions of it over time. Printing of Money can also make nations to be uncompetitive and less productive on a global scale.

Then the Governments and Central Banks are able to buy the assets that have plummeted; by buying up the assets, this helps to drive up the asset's prices, but this only helps people who have real financial assets like Rental incomes, REIT's, Gold, Silver, Essential Businesses, etc. The Central Banks can only buy financial assets, not goods and services, so in order to support the economy at large, the Central Banks buy Government bonds, which gives the Government the ability to buy goods and services. This, then, in turn, gets the money that was printed to stimulate the economy into the hands of people at large and not just financial assets.

The Government can now run at a deficit while also spending on stimulus programs and unemployment benefits. This will lower the economy's overall Debt burden over time and increase spending and incomes. This will then run its full course until the economy reaches another economic bubble again.

Government policymakers, world leaders, and presidents need to balance the Four Levers effectively in order to lead an Effective and Efficient Deleveraging. When the Four Levers are used efficiently, Debt declines relative to Income growth, real economic growth is positive, and inflation isn't a problem. This result is achieved because a delicate surgical balance between spending, reducing debt, transferring wealth, and printing money is maintained.

Printing of Money won't necessarily lead to inflation provided it offsets the decrease in Credit but does not exceed it.

But if too much money is printed, it can lead to Hyper-Inflation, which is what Germany experienced during its Deleveraging in the 1920s when 160 German marks were equivalent to just one US dollar.[23] An ugly Deleveraging occurs if Income growth is not higher than the rate of interest accumulated on Debt to cut the Debt burden.

The Reflation or Recovery phase of the Long-term Debt cycle, which is the time it takes for Debt Burdens to fall and economic activity to resume as usual, lasts roughly 7 to 10 years (10 years for the Great Depression and 7 for the global financial crisis), this is known as a Lost Decade.

THREE RULES OF THUMB TO NAVIGATE THE ECONOMY

We owe ourselves the responsibility to ensure that we manage our finances and national economy effectively by making the right choices, taking the best long-term decisions, delaying gratification, being productive, and creating lasting value and impact in our society, whether through our own businesses or organizations that we work for.

We can also personally adopt this Three thumb rule of Ray Dalio for our personal life:

1. Don't let Debt rise faster than Income (Debt Burdens will eventually crush you)
2. Don't have Income (spendings) rise faster than Productivity (value creation, production of goods and services) -- it will eventually render you uncompetitive.
3. Do all you can to raise Productivity – this is what matters the most in the long run.

CHAPTER 3
THE IDEA THAT BIRTHS BITCOIN & BLOCKCHAIN TECHNOLOGY

In the wake of the Global economic crisis that happened in 2008, which left many people, businesses, corporations, and governments devasted, depressed, and in debt due to the failings, errors, inadequacies, lapses, misappropriation of funds, and shortcomings of the world's financial system, central banks, and financial institutions. Also, due to the fact that many country's economy is driven by Debt and Credit systems, as explained in an earlier chapter, the large defaulting in debts by People who are unable to pay back the risk loans that were given out by many banks was also part of the trigger of this global economic crash.

Banks lost money from their investments in various projects and opportunities; these investments did not generate enough returns, and Banks lost their customer's money that was kept in their trust and security. There was a widespread declaration of Bankruptcy by many of these banks, and the governments of these countries had to come to their rescue with bailouts, including the American Government. Most of these Banks lost the money that the People had entrusted in their care, and with no way for the People to recover the money back, they literally lost their wealth.

The funny part of this situation was that the bailout (the rescue money) that the Governments were giving the Banks to save them from collapse and bankruptcy was also the People's money, which had been paid in Taxes. Since the Global economy is interconnected, the economic events that took place in the USA reverberated all over the world, bringing the world's economy to a standstill. This global financial crisis brought out a lot of problems associated with the World's Banking and Financial System that operates by a Central Authority that cannot be trusted.

HOW YOUR GOVERNMENT AFFECTS YOUR MONEY & WEALTH

The Government of your country spends the People's money for the welfare, infrastructure, and socioeconomic development of the Nation and its people. The Government receives money from various types of taxes that people pay and from other means of internally generated revenue from its natural resources, international trade, export and import of goods and services, investment in various infrastructural projects, etc. It happens that in most cases all over the world, the expenditure of the Government exceeds its income; in order to deal with this in relation to the Country's Debt profile and Economic state (high inflation rates, high unemployment, etc.), the Government ask the Central Bank to print more money. This way, the Government tries to make the money available to the public. The Government has no fixed limit to the amount of money it can print into the economy, thereby causing devaluation of the nation's currency, reducing the currency purchasing power, and yet leading to inflation (high price of goods and services).

Let me explain this for you in simple math, assuming there is $100 dollars in circulation in the country, and you own $1 dollar. This would mean that you own 1% of the money in your country. If the Government prints more money and now the total amount of money in circulation goes up to $200 dollars, the value of your money (wealth) would go down to 0.5% of the entire market share. That's a 50% decrease in the value of your money (wealth) saved in the Banks. These are just in plain mathematical terms, but the concept remains the same and the value of your money goes down and depreciates anytime the Government spends more money than it earns, borrows money unendingly, increases its national debt limits, and gives the Central Bank of the country authority to prints more money.

As a result of all these shortcomings in the world's financial system, we are forced to work incessantly all our lives to earn money, so that the decrease in the value of money (devaluation) and loss of its purchasing power in the economy of our nation won't affect us too much, yet we can barely keep up with the rat race. We lose our money and wealth faster than we make and create it, to Inflation (rising cost of goods and services), debt crisis, bank's bankruptcy, economic crisis, devaluation of currencies, and many more.

THE IDEA THAT BIRTH BITCOIN & BLOCKCHAIN TECHNOLOGY

All these financial problems, wealth creation, and preservation challenges above are what stirred up the very idea that gave birth to Bitcoin. People's hearts yearned for a solution, a way out of the financial mess that the world has found itself in, and like the wise quote of Martha Beck that says, "Any deep crisis moment creates an opportunity to make your life extraordinary in some way." People wanted a currency, a medium of exchange that would not be controlled by a Central Authority, a government, or any Central Banks.

Amid all this global financial crisis, a man or team by the pseudonym "Satoshi Nakamoto" developed the first Bitcoin software and introduced the concept of cryptocurrency to the world in a 2008 whitepaper. Satoshi Nakamoto remained active in the creation of Bitcoin and the blockchain technology until about 2010 but has not been since then (this could be one of his personal security measures against the powerful elites, governments, oligarchs, central banks, and world leaders who would have want to hurt him and his vision of birthing a globalized, decentralized currency that preserves wealth for the good, well-being and welfare of everyone).

Satoshi Nakamoto was not the first to hit on the idea of cryptocurrency, but he was the one to solve a fundamental problem that prevented its adoption: unlike paper currency, cryptocurrency could be duplicated. This was known as "Double Spending," and Nakamoto solved it by creating the blockchain system of verification. He published a bitcoin whitepaper titled, "Bitcoin: A Peer-to-Peer Electronic Cash System.".[24] Satoshi Nakamoto proposed a decentralized approach for transactions using ledgers, a network, Merkle roots and trees, timestamps, incentives, cryptography, and a consensus mechanism.[25]

In a blockchain, timestamps are added to transaction information, and cryptographic techniques are used to encrypt the data. The encrypted data cannot be changed but must be validated. The network must verify the authenticity of the transactions based on a majority consensus mechanism called Proof-of-Work.

This record of transactions is distributed across many nodes in the system, it is difficult, if not impossible, for a bad actor to gain control enough of the system to rewrite the ledger to their advantage. The blockchain records are kept secure because the computational power required to reverse them discourages small-scale attacks. Hackers would need a network that could validate and create blocks faster than the current network at the right time to overwrite it. They'd also need to deploy several other blockchain attacks at the same time, and even with all these, they still can't beat the Proof-of-Work blockchain technology.

The Bitcoin Blockchain Technology also helped to tackle and solve the third-party intermediaries' trust issues and difficulties. In most cases, third parties, such as Banks and Financial institutions could effectively handle transactions without adding significant risk. However, this trust-based model still results in additional costs and the risk of fraud.

In the past, trusted third parties have proven to be unworthy of the trust placed in them. It does not necessarily have to be the Institutions themselves that provide the third-party validation services that are untrustworthy, but the very people involved in the transactions that cannot be Trusted. Thus, there is a need to remove the human factor altogether. Cryptography and automated group consensus mechanisms are currently the only way to get around human intervention in finances.

Bitcoin also addressed the challenge of excessive money printing by Central Banks and Governments into the economy, thereby devaluing our currency and reducing its purchasing power. Bitcoin solved this problem by fixing the maximum number of Bitcoins that could ever be in circulation and the rate at which new Bitcoins would be produced. The maximum number and the rate of production cannot go beyond the set limit because of the coding used in its design. In order to ensure that more Bitcoins can't be mined, the blockchain ledger and technology are made available, visible, and transparent to all for easy verification.

The Price and Value of each Bitcoin are also dependent and determined on the supply and demand in the market and are free from all kinds of Government intervention, like when the Government artificially alters the price and value of a currency for various reasons.

BITCOIN WALLET

Saving your physical fiat money in the bank requires that you have or open a Bank account with all the valid documents required for the process. When your account is open, you pay the money into your account, and when the Bank's Teller receives it from you or through an electronic transfer payment, the said amount will be credited and written against your name in your bank account. This leaves your money (wealth) in the direct control of Banks, Central Authority, and Governments, but with your personal Bitcoin wallet, you are the sole custodian of your own money and wealth, and it is secured, protected, and safe with you even more than it could ever have been in any banks in this world as long as you keep your Bitcoin wallet 12 security words save and secured from being compromised by anybody and you can transfer value (money) to anybody in the world via your Bitcoin wallet. All the way from Singapore to Brazil, from China to the USA, from Japan to Nigeria, from Rwanda to France, from Switzerland to Turkey, all across the globe, you can transfer value (money, wealth, digital assets) at the snap of your finger without any third-party interfering and expensive fees or charges.

BITCOIN'S FACTS, NUMBERS & TOKENOMICS

There can ONLY be 21 million Bitcoins that can ever be produced. It has been built into the coin's code or DNA. As of today, 19.4 million have been mined, although some of them are already lost. According to crypto data from Chainalysis, around 20% of Bitcoin has been lost or stuck in wallets that can't be accessed. This equates to 3.76 million BTC. The way Bitcoin mining works, the number of Bitcoins that can be mined gets halved every four years; this means that although almost 90% of the total possible Bitcoin already in circulation has been mined, it will still take almost another 120 years (year 2140 to be precise) to produce the remaining 1.6 million coins.

The lowest denomination of Bitcoin is a Satoshi; there are 100 million Satoshi in a Bitcoin. This means that 100 Sat is equivalent to 0.000001, and 1,000,000 Sat is equivalent to 0.01 Bitcoin. The denomination was named after the developer of Bitcoin and Blockchain Technology, Satoshi Nakamoto. This allows easy understanding of small amounts of Bitcoin because the cryptocurrency commands such a high value. The First ever commercial transaction done with Bitcoin was carried out on May 22, 2010, by Laszlo Hanyecz, who paid 10,000 BTC for two Papa John's Pizzas worth about $41 dollars at the time. This date is commemorated as the Bitcoin Pizza's Day each year. At today's price, that 10,000 BTC would be worth over $260 million dollars (current price at average $26,000) at the peak of the Bull market in Nov. 2021 when the price for a unit BTC was $69,000 dollars as it's All Time High. The 10,000 BTC would have been worth over $690 million dollars, which is perhaps the reason why the story has become a part of Bitcoin folklore.

It is difficult to know for sure how many Bitcoin millionaires or billionaires there are in the world today because Bitcoin Wallets are anonymous, and the price of Bitcoin fluctuates, sometimes wildly. However according to BitInfoCharts, there are currently over 100,000 addresses with BTC worth $1 million dollars or more in them. Forbes included 12 cryptocurrency billionaires on its 2021 Billionaires list, which includes the Winklevoss Twins, Michael Saylor, and Tim Draper.

THE BUDDING BLOCKCHAIN TECHNOLOGY

The advent of the Bitcoin's blockchain technology, "Proof-of-Work" (PoW), has led to the rise of development and innovation of other faster, larger, scalable blockchain technology like Proof of Stake (PoS) with Smart Contracts, etc. And other Cryptocurrency like Ethereum (ETH), Ripple (XRP), Solana (SOL), Dogecoin (DOGE), Binance Chain (BNB), and many more with various user cases, chain layers, sectors (Smart contracts. DeFi, NFT's, Games, etc.), utility, adoption and unique problems they are trying to solve. While some are even just for fun, entertainment, and educational purposes, they are called Meme coins like Shiba Inu, Pepe, WikiCat, etc.

As of today, we have over 22,000 different cryptocurrencies that fall under the different categories listed above.[26] Although, over 80% of these may not stay on the scene for long because of the ever increasing technological growth, progress, and competition in the Crypto Industry that gives rise to new Blockchain solutions and tokens being developed. The Crypto Industry is still very, very early, young, and budding with very little or no regulation around it yet in many countries. As a result of this, there have been some bad and fraudulent players in the industry that have led to the loss of money, business and the collapse of corporations.

For example, players like Sam Bankman Fried (SBF), the founder and developer of FTX token that, mismanaged people's funds which led to the collapse of the Token and loss of customer's money to the tune of $8 Billion dollars,[27] and the filing of Bankruptcy for His two companies FTX Trading Ltd, a crypto exchange platform and Almeda Research, a quantitative trading firm, that was worth $32 Billion dollars.[28] The then 30-year-old SBF was said to have committed one of the biggest financial frauds in US History, and the contagion effects of this gross financial misconduct really affected a lot of people's money and wealth in the Digital Assets and Crypto Industry space.[29]

Another example of bad and fraudulent players in the very young, budding Crypto Blockchain Industry is Do Kwon, a South Korean entrepreneur, the founder of the Terra token and LUNA token that lost over $40 Billion dollars[30] of people's money and institutional investors wealth after the collapse of the tokens He developed, TerraUSD and LUNA.[31] This very sad, devastating loss of funds and wealth is a result of the irresponsible behaviors, bad choices, bad decisions, and actions of these bad players. All of these have led to the call for Regulation, Quality control, Proof of Research, and Investigative works to be carried out on top-tier crypto companies, platforms, their founders, and CEO's by several countries all across the globe.

There has been a lot of debate around whether Bitcoin should be the only accredited cryptocurrency in the world because it was mathematically developed and originally programmed to avoid situations and circumstances like the ones mentioned above that cause loss of money, wealth and devastating situations for people and businesses. The Securities and Exchange Commission, SEC of the United States of America, has also rightly argued that Bitcoin (BTC) is duly recognized as a commodity, a digital asset with no issuer, that is valuable, trusted, and demanded globally.[32] However, it categorizes other cryptocurrencies, all known as Altcoins, under Securities for them to be able to control and regulate them, although this is not totally correct, and there are cases in courts between the SEC and the founders or CEOs of these various Digital Assets (Cryptocurrencies, Tokens, Coins, etc.) on where to draw the line between securities, commodities, and transparent regulation of the Crypto Blockchain industry.[33]

ADOPTION AND IMPACT OF BLOCKCHAIN TECHNOLOGY

The very idea of Blockchain Technology was first conceived and used as the mechanism to support Bitcoin, to solve the problem associated with digital currencies. Satoshi Nakamoto devised an immutable ledger of transactions that chains together blocks of data using digital cryptography. This new technology is now gaining adoption and is used widely by some key industries and sectors of the Economy of nations around the world.

BANKS & FINANCIAL HOUSES

A lot of big banks and financial houses are now using the Blockchain Technology for fast bank money transfers and payments because it is way faster than their current existing money transfer services and payment systems, which usually would take 2 to 3 days, especially for cross-border transactions, but now within minutes value (money) can be transferred between customers without much hassle and stress.

INSURANCE COMPANIES

The use of Smart contracts on the Blockchain technology provides a very high level of transparency for customers and insurance providers (for their property, cars, assets, and life). A well-recorded and documented claim has helped customers and insurance companies resolve their disputes and duplicate claims for the same event. Also, the use of smart contracts also helps to speed up the process for claimants to receive payments. Hence, the increasing adoption of the Blockchain Technology in the Insurance industry.

REAL ESTATE FIRMS

The ever-growing and booming Real Estate industry requires a ton of paperwork, documentation, and verification of financial information and the transfer of deeds and titles to new owners. The use of blockchain technology by top real estate firms has helped to provide a more secure, easily accessible means of verifying documents and transfer of ownership. This has helped to increase the speed and service delivery time, operational cost, no cumbersome paperwork, and increase value addition to their companies.

GOVERNMENT HOUSES AND PARASTATALS

It's amazing how some countries like El Salvador and Central African Republic have adopted Bitcoin as a legal tender for their nation, and this has revolutionized their nation's finances and economy, the welfare of their citizens, tourists, and immigrants in a great way. We will discuss more about this in future chapters as more and more countries are making plans to adopt Bitcoin as a legal tender in their country.[34]

Also, a lot of government houses and parastatals are now using the blockchain technology in the administration of their government's welfare programs, social security, Medicare, and palliatives. The use of the blockchain technology has helped to reduce fraud, mismanagement of resources, wastage, and the cost of operations for these governments' programs. Beneficiaries also received their benefits timely through digital disbursement on the blockchain system.

HOSPITALS AND PHARMACEUTICAL COMPANIES

There is a growing adoption of the use of Blockchain Technology in the field of Medicine, as many hospitals and pharmaceutical companies are now using the blockchain technology to obtain accurate and up-to-date information on their patients, the right analysis and correlation of patterns among their patients, and the drugs they are researching about. Also, the adoption of the blockchain technology has helped to ensure that patients seeing multiple doctors can get the best care possible. All of the patient's records are held in the database for doctors to easily review and verify if the patient is registered under a medical insurance scheme and their treatment is covered.

LOGISTICS, SHIPPING AND SUPPLY CHAIN COMPANIES

Lots of Shipping companies and Supply chain firms are now using the Blockchain Technology to monitor and track their items as they move through logistics and supply chain networks. It has helped to provide greater ease of communication between partners since data is available on a secure public ledger. Also, most shipping and supply chain firms are now using the blockchain technology because it provides greater security and data integrity, as data on the chain cannot be altered or manipulated by any party. This has helped to increase the trust level, collaboration, and partnerships of major players in the shipping and supply chain industry all over the world, leading to more value creation and an economic boost.

Other Industries where the Blockchain technology is also experiencing fast adoption growth are Music & Entertainment for royalties and streaming services, Electoral Voting process, NFT's (Non-Fungible Tokens), Lending, etc. The Blockchain Technology is still in its infancy stage and has only been around for a dozen years, and businesses are still exploring new ways to adopt and apply the technology to support their operations and scale their business growth. There is going to be a continued steady rise in the adoption and application of this new technology in every aspect of our lives, just as we did with the use of the Internet and social media networks. As digital data is used in our personal lives, businesses, governments, banks, and countries continue to increase exponentially. There is going to be a constant growing need for the data security, access, transparency, and integrity that the Blockchain Technology provides to everyone.

CHAPTER 4
OG'S AND FOUNDERS OF CRYPTO INDUSTRY

Every well-known, impactful field, great ideas, powerful inventions, and established institution and industry in the world has its pioneers, founding fathers, and intellectual giants that blazed the trail and set the pace for others to follow. In the Crypto Industry, we call them OG's and Founders, and in this chapter, we will be looking at the men who have really championed the cause for financial freedom, transparency, growth, and adoption of Cryptocurrencies, made a lasting impact, and mark in the Crypto Industry. The very industry that is now giving rise and birth to new millionaires and billionaires as they take advantage of the new blockchain technology that has leveled the playing field for both the ordinary, downtrodden people and the elites, royal people in their palaces and mansions.

Of course, the very first person on the list is no other person than Satoshi Nakamoto, whom we have discussed quite extensively about in preceding chapters. We'll be talking about some key vital players in the crypto industry that you may know or might not have heard of before, that have made great exploits in the Crypto Industry and Digital Assets space. Unlike the rich and powerful in the regular traditional finance and conventional tech sector, Crypto OGs are often protected by a layer of decentralized anonymity in the wild cyberspace.

They founded or joined successful crypto blockchain projects at the right time, which got bigger and more reputable over time to become full companies and organizations that employees hundreds and thousands of employees, working both on-site and remotely. Anyone serious about Cryptocurrency and Blockchain Technology ought to know their names, their works, and their biographies in order to learn a thing or two that will greatly improve their lives.

SATOSHI NAKAMOTO

He is often referred to as the Father of Bitcoin or Cryptocurrency for his ingenuity and courage to develop the first Blockchain technology database. He is the author of the Bitcoin Whitepaper. Analysis of Bitcoin's blockchain has helped deduce which addresses are likely Satoshi Nakamoto's to a relatively high degree of certainty, according to chain analysis from Sergio Demian Lerner, the chief scientist of RSK Labs, Satoshi Nakamoto has around 1 million Bitcoin. These addresses date back to the beginning of Bitcoin in 2008. While the very identity of Satoshi Nakamoto has not been attributed to anyone, it is estimated that the value of Bitcoins in Satoshi Nakamoto's portfolio is very significant. The 1 million Bitcoins in is portfolio is worth over $25 Billion dollars as at today's current price value of $25,769 per unit BTC.[35]

VITALIK BUTERIN

Vitalik Buterin does not have the enigmatic mystery of the anonymous founder of Bitcoin, Satoshi Nakamoto, but He is one of the OGs and founders of crypto. Vitalik Buterin is a Russian-Canadian computer programmer and developer. He is the co-founder of Ethereum (ETH), the second largest cryptocurrency in the world with a market capitalization of over $195 Billion dollars as at today's current price value of $1,631 per unit ETH.[36] But beyond its dominant market position, Vitalik Buterin showed the world that Crypto can be more than just a store of value (wealth) or a means of exchange (money). He developed a blockchain technology with a different paradigm of distributed computing and smart contracts. Vitalik's technological innovations, talents as a writer, programmer, philosophy, and mission are to lead cryptocurrency and financial markets as a whole out of the woods and shadows to Blockchains's light.

He began laying the blocks for Ethereum's foundation in 2013 when he was just 19 years old and wrote a white paper that outlined "a next-generation smart contract and decentralized application platform." Buterin's work took the groundbreaking development of Bitcoin's underlying blockchain technology to the next level. He saw the vision of how Blockchain Technology could build different platforms with even greater possibilities driven by His smart contract blockchain.

A smart contract is a self-executing program whose terms and rules are encoded on a Blockchain. Think of the Uber APP on your smartphone, minus both the Uber company and your phone. Smart contracts aim to ditch intermediaries of all kinds, enabling seamless, automatic, trackable, and irreversible agreements between any parties. Vitalik's idea is to use Blockchain-based smart contracts to encode all the assets and bylaws of entire organizations, allowing them to function without independent oversight.

Vitalik's Ethereum was the first smart contract platform in the world when it was launched in July 2015; since then, the Blockchain platform has launched a host of decentralized applications, including the first ever decentralized lending protocol known as MakerDAO, Decentraland (MANA) a crypto gaming initiative, and the NFT Marketplace OpenSea, and many more.

JOSEPH LUBIN

Joseph Lubin is a Canadian American Entrepreneur. He has founded and co-founded several companies, including Swiss Based EthSuisse. He contributed heavily to Ethereum, the Decentralized Cryptocurrency platform. Lubin is also the founder of ConsenSys, a Brooklyn-based blockchain software technology company. As of February 2018 Forbes estimated Lubin's net worth in Cryptocurrency to be between One to Five Billion dollars.[37] Lubin's ConsenSys company also develops decentralized software services for companies, and he is personally involved in cross-industry groups attempting to advance solutions to governance issues in the Blockchain industry.

THE WINKLEVOSS TWINS

The Winklevoss Twins, Cameron and Tyler Winklevoss are well known in the tech world as the guys who had the pioneering idea that birthed the social media network giant called Facebook, which was later founded by Mark Zuckerberg, the parent company of Meta, now worth over $760 Billion today.[38] Although, they were later settled in court with $65 million in cash and Facebook stock in 2008 over the creation of the social media network.[39] The Twin Brothers established their family office called Winklevoss Capital in 2012 and started amassing large amounts of Bitcoin when the price was still very much undervalued, less than a single digit.[40]

The Winklevoss Twins owned as much as 1% of the circulating supply of Bitcoin as of November 2013, according to the Washinton Post.[41] They went on from buying up a stash of

Bitcoin to being the first people to ever launch a Bitcoin ETF (or exchange-traded fund), which was rejected by SEC, which has now become a hot cake that many leading Global Asset Management firms like Blackrock, Fidelity, Ark Invest, Grayscale, etc. as they are now vying for it and submitting several Bitcoin ETF applications to the SEC.[42] In 2015, the Winklevoss brothers founded Gemini, a cryptocurrency exchange licensed in its home state of New York that processes about $70 Million dollars a day in trades.[43]

The Crypto Exchange platform expanded over the years and acquired NFT marketplace Nifty Gateway in 2019, ahead of the eventual NFT market boom in 2021. Their Parent company, Gemini Space Station, was valued at $7.1 Billion dollars as of November 2021. Cameron and Tyler were deemed Bitcoin Billionaires in 2017, as chronicled in Ben Mezrich's book, as the price of Bitcoin surged to nearly $20,000 during the Bull run. Forbes recently estimated each brother to have a net worth of $1.5 Billion.[44]

JIHAN WU

For you to be a legend in the Crypto Industry with a credible impact and pedigree can go through many routes, you don't necessarily have to be a genius programmer or venture capitalist. For Jihan Wu, it was done through the mining of Bitcoin. Jihan Wu is a Chinese Crypto Entrepreneur; together with Micree Zhan, they co-founded Bitmain Technologies in 2013 which has now become the World's largest computer chip company for Bitcoin Mining, with $2.5 Billion revenue in 2017. He is also a leading financier of the Crypto Token called Bitcoin Cash, a hard fork of Bitcoin created in 2017 with increased transaction capacity. Jihan Wu topped Forbes' 2020 World's Billionaires list as one of the five youngest Billionaires in Asia.[45]

CHANGPENG ZHAO CZ

Changpeng Zhao, popularly known as CZ, is a Chinese born Canadian Businessman, Investor, and Software Engineer. Zhao is the co-founder and CEO of Binance, the world's largest Cryptocurrency Exchange by trading volume as of July 2022.[46] According to Bloomberg Billionaires Index, CZ was ranked the 136th richest person in the world with a net worth estimated at $13.1 Billion as of December 2022.[47]

CZ is one of the leading pioneers and visionaries in the Crypto industry with his keen, sagacious, and innovative mind focused on creating real-world utility products and services for people all around the world with varieties of Blockchain products, services, payments systems, functionalities, and creating a sound Crypto Ecosystem. With Blockchain products like Binance Card, Binance Pay, Binance Market Place, Binance NFT, Binance Earn, Binance Academy, Binance Launchpad, etc.

MICHAEL SAYLOR

Michael Saylor is an American Entrepreneur and a former Rocket scientist. Saylor studied aeronautics and astronautics at MIT on an Airforce scholarship before founding MicroStrategy in 1989 and becoming a business executive. He is the executive chairman and co-founder of MicroStrategy, a company that provides business intelligence, mobile software, and cloud-based services. Saylor served as MicroStrategy's CEO from 1989 to 2022. He wrote titled, "The Mobile Wave: How Mobile Intelligence Will Change Everything." He is also the sole trustee of Saylor Academy, a free online academy that is focused on educating people about Bitcoin and its importance. As of 2016, Saylor has been granted 31 patents, and 9 additional under review.[48]

Michael Saylor's strategic impact in the Crypto industry is his voice as a strong advocate for Bitcoin Adoption as the store of value, wealth, and reserve for individuals, institutional investors, governments, and corporations. He adopted Bitcoin for his company's coffers and reserve and bought 17,732 Bitcoins for $175 million in 2020. He has been very consistent with this Bitcoin Adoption strategy and keeps accumulating the total amount of Bitcoin in circulation at rapid DCA (Dollar Cost Average) during either peak or low market seasons. As of today, Michael Saylor's MicroStrategy company is holding 152,800 Bitcoin with a total purchase value of $4.53 Billion dollars at an average price of $29,672.[49] This has greatly helped the stocks and shares value of the Company as it is 92% correlated to Bitcoin over the last 3 years (2020-2023).[50]

CHRIS LARSEN

Chris Larsen is an American business executive and angel investor reputed for founding several Silicon Valley technology startups, including one based on peer-to-peer lending. In 1996, He co-founded the online mortgage lender E-Loan, and during his tenure as CEO, the company became the first company to freely provide consumers FICO credit scores. By 2000, E-Loan's market value was estimated at $1 Billion dollars. In 2012, He co-founded the company called Ripple Labs Inc., which developed Ripple (XRP), a blockchain software that enables the instant and direct transfer of money between two parties using Blockchain Technology.[51]

As of today, the market value of the token Ripple (XRP) used on Chris Larsen's blockchain software is $26 Billion dollars, with the unit price of Ripple token (XRP) at $0.4984.[52] On January 4, 2018, Forbes estimated that Chris Larsen's worth at $59 Billion dollars, briefly putting him ahead of Mark Zuckerberg and into the fifth place in their list of world's richest people.[53] In 2020, He ranked No. 319 in the Forbes 400 list of the richest people in America.[54]

TIM DRAPER

Tim Draper is a scion of Silicon Valley investing dynasty. He is the third in a familial line of venture capitalists and government officials. He is the founding partner of Venture Capital firm Draper Fisher Jurvetson. His most prominent investments include Tesla, SpaceX, Baidu, Hotmail, Skype, Twitter (now known as X), Coinbase, Robinhood, Twitch, Cruise Automation, Angel List, Solar City, Ancestry.com, and Focus Media. In July 2014, Tim Draper received wide coverage for His purchase of 29,656 Bitcoins seized by US Marshals service from the Silk Road website for $18.7 Million dollars at $632 dollars per Bitcoin.[55] As of today's current market value, these 29,656 Bitcoins are now worth a staggering $763.3 million dollars at $25,740 per unit,[56] that's a profit yield percentage of over 3,950%. Tim Draper strongly believes that the price of Bitcoin will continue to rise in value over time due to its deflationary mechanism and blockchain programming. He predicts that the price of a unit of Bitcoin will be around $250,000 by 2025.[57]

MICHAEL NOVOGRATZ

Michael Novogratz is an American investor; he is one of the people who took Fortress Investment Group public in 2007. He is currently the CEO of Galaxy Investment Partners, which focuses on investments in Cryptocurrency. As of today, the multi-strategy crypto investment firm is worth over $650 Million dollars.[58] In 2017, Novogratz said that 20% of His net worth is in Bitcoin and Ethereum and that He made $250 million dollars from Cryptocurrency between 2016 and 2017 during the bull run market.[59] Of recent, in 2021, Michael Novogratz owns $4.8 Billion dollars of Cryptocurrency, and it makes 85% of His wealth.[60] His company, Galaxy Investments, lost $77 Million dollar as a result of FTX collapse. He also appeared in the movie series titled Billions as Himself.[61]

ROGER VER

In the world of Cryptocurrency, it's rare to find a major player who isn't also controversial. Roger Ver is exactly that type of Individual. He is one of the earliest, most vocal proponents of and investors in Cryptocurrency and several Crypto-related startups, including Ripple (XRP), Blockchain.com, and Bitcoin.-com.[62] He gained the nickname "Bitcoin Jesus" for his opinions, views, and advocacy for Bitcoin. Roger Ver was an early adopter of the first digital currency, Bitcoin. He integrated Bitcoin payments into Memorydealers.com, allowing customers to make payments in Bitcoin. By adopting the payment method in the early days when Bitcoin was valued at under $1, Roger Ver amassed a total collection of more than 400,000 Bitcoins by some estimates.[63] In the process of advocacy for Bitcoin, it's like His Bitcoin collection was reduced through payments and funding projects.

BILL MILLER

Bill Miller is an American Value Investor, Fund Manager, and Philanthropist. Bill Miller gained prominence for His investment expertise for outperforming the S&P 500 annually from 1991 to 2005. He is the Chairman and Chief Investment Officer of Miller Value Partners, which has $1.9 Billion dollars under assets as of the end of August 2022. In January 2023, Miller announced that he would retire at the end of the year, outlining his succession plans for his two main funds, transferring management to his son, Bill Miller IV, and longtime protégé

Samantha McLemore. Bill Miller famously bought Amazon at the company's IPO in 1997.

The famed Value Investor is a strong advocate for Bitcoin and Cryptocurrency, as he has some of his portfolios holding Bitcoin to hedge against financial crisis because it is not strongly connected to the world's financial system [64] Bill Miller said that he has 50% of his personal wealth in Bitcoin, and He was buying the valued global digital assets as of 2014 when the price was at $200.[65] Bill Miller believes Bitcoin is best thought of as "Digital Gold" with a strictly limited supply and He allows himself to be called a "Bitcoin Bull" rather than an observer because it has developed into a game-changing technology.[66]

SIR MAPY

Sir Mapy is a pseudonym name for one of Africa's brightest minds in the Crypto space, who is revolutionizing and advocating for the strong use of blockchain technology for the socio-economic development, education, and cryptocurrency adoption for youth's empowerment and financial freedom in Nigeria, Ghana, South Africa.[67] He is the founder of SMC DAO, a Decentralized Organization focused on building a community of crypto believers focused on building wealth, transforming their community, and creating innovations through the digital economy. SMC DAO has over 50,000+ Crypto and blockchain technology advocates. SMC DAO is also the parent founder of the dominant crypto token called Wiki Cat (WKC), a denounced crypto project that was created to teach young Africans about cryptocurrency and blockchain technology.[68]

Despite the challenges and difficulties of running a successful enterprise in Africa, Sir Mapy and His SMC DAO community have been able to change the financial sector and economy of countries like Nigeria, Ghana, South Africa, etc. Sir Mapy is renowned as one of the pioneering legends who bought the meme token Shiba Inu with $500 and made almost $480,000 from it, with several other crypto projects like Transhuman coin, Kishu Inu, etc., and a cumulative of almost $600,000 during the Crypto market bull run of 2021.

We've taken enough time to go through the stories and profiles of great men who have made valuable impacts, contributions, and growth to their nation's economies with a good legacy because just as the famous, wise old sage, the richest and greatest investor that ever lived in modern history, Warren Buffet, also known as the Oracle of Omaha said, "Tell me who your Heroes are, and I will tell you how you are going to turn out to be. The Best thing I did was choose the right heroes." All these Heroes and many more out there are heroes in the Cryptocurrency and blockchain technology world that you can draw inspiration, courage and wisdom from to be a Hero like them too in your community and world.

THE REVOLUTION OF BITCOIN AND BLOCKCHAIN TECHNOLOGY

Over centuries and thousands of years, we humans have grown to develop various means of survival, adaptation, innovation, creativity, cutting-edge technologies, wealth creation, and wealth preservation measures with different methodologies and pathways to financial freedom, greatness, and abundance, right from the agrarian age to the industrial age to the information age. We forget to realize how far we've come as humans over these long centuries and thousands of years to where we are today. How many privileges, loads of advantages, and opportunities are we enjoying today that we might even be taking for granted? The advent of Electricity, X-Ray machines, Modern health and medicine, science advancement, Instant messaging, and communication systems, Internet, Airplanes, and several other things we now use in our day-to-day life that we enjoy as norms were all wild dreams, hopes, and impossible luxuries for those who lived hundreds of years before us.

When we think of wealth today, we often think of the massive personal fortunes amassed by Business Magnates like Bill Gates, Jeff Bezos, Elon Musk, or Warren Buffet. Yet we miss out on the fact that it's only since the Industrial evolution that measuring wealth by one's bank account and acclaimed net worth has been a norm for the world's richest. For most of human history, the lines around wealth were quite blurred. Leaders like Augustus Caesar or Emperor Shenzong had complete control of empires, while bankers like Jacob Fogger and Cosimo de Medici were often pulling strings from behind the scenes.

During early times, wealth was tied to Land (Genghis Khan), livestock, cattle, oxen, gold, silver, purple garments, precious stones, spoils of war, and war conquest for empires like Augustus Caesar, William the Conqueror, who conquered large empires and had tons of massive gold. For us to be wealthy during these times, we would most likely have to be born into a family with great wealth and influence, or we would grow up to become great warriors ourselves who would conquer territories.

Then came the time of the great industrial revolution and the exploits of the great men and women who built wealth and abundance from nothing by taking advantage of the new inventions and industrial revolution that was ongoing during their time in the 1800's. Men like John D Rockefeller, Cornelius Vanderbilt, Henry Ford, and Andrew Carnegie were the great tycoons and wealthy men of those times. They were captains of Industries, business magnates, titans, and capitalists. The Wealth during their time also highlighted the vast financial inequality between them and the middle class (employees of their various chains of industries) and low-income earners.

This is so largely because it requires a great deal of resources, time, expertise, and a combination of various factors of labor to build wealth and abundance, which is not so commonly readily available for low- and middle-class people. Building of railroads, factories, steel companies, coal, and mining industries involves a lot of strategic resources, management, funding, logistics, supply chain, and distribution of the goods and services to the end users. Big Businesses boomed with the creation of technology such as typewriters, cash registers, and adding machines that helped to transform how people worked. During this time of great expansion, there were fewer regulations surrounding wealth and business practice, circumstances were perfect for the rise of the extremely wealthy individuals who made up a very small percentage of society. Although they had the power and means to create opportunities and jobs for many, with less prioritization of worker's rights, issues like discrimination, exploitation, and low wages marked these times.

Then, as time progressed, we've been privileged to watch the rise and accumulation of wealth of men like Bill Gates, Jeff Bezos, Larry Page, Michael Bloomberg, Sergey Brin, Bernard Arnault, Warren Buffet, Richard Branson, Mark Zuckerberg, etc. who through the advent of the internet, better technologies that helped to build businesses around the web created fortunes and amassed wealth and abundance, even though they didn't inherit their wealth.

Building wealth has been a smoother ride for baby boomers, who inherited a sweeter deal than the younger generations that came after these Tech moguls and businessmen. Millennials and Gen Z have had a much harder time building wealth due to a lot of student debts, stagnant wages, and ill-timed recessions caused by economic crashes and global financial crises. Achieving the American dream and financial freedom are now more difficult, especially with the challenging housing market where many believe their dreams of one day buying their own home to be impossible. Whereas most baby boomers had their own share of rising inflation and economic challenges, the economy was more like a game set on easy mode for their generation that benefited from less expensive education as well as lower interest rates and inflated housing prices that made them build assets more easily.

Making it seem like more humans are advancing in their economic growth, monetary theories, social relationships management, technological development, and advancement, the harder it is to become financially free and wealthy. We can go on and on talking about the different challenges and opportunities that we've faced in different times and eras as humans, but we need to understand that just as Charles Dickens stated in the Tale of Two Cities, "It was the best of times, it was the worst of times, it was the age of wisdom, it was the age of foolishness, it was the epoch of belief, it was the epoch of incredulity, it was the season of light, it was the season of darkness, it was the spring of hope, it was the winter of despair."

Just as we've rightly pointed out in the last chapter on the new set of Heroes that are rising from the crypto and blockchain industry based on the advent of Bitcoin and Blockchain technology, we can draw inspiration, courage, and wisdom from their lives to also go ahead and build our own America dreams with financial freedom and wealth. We don't have to settle with the status quo and keep living in mediocrity, barely surviving on government handouts and bailouts. We can build our own wealth dynasty and make a lasting and valuable impact in the lives of our loved ones, family, colleagues, community, society, and the world at large.

Bitcoin and Blockchain have indeed helped to revolutionize how we can create wealth and achieve financial freedom for ourselves and our families without having to depend on our states or governments to empower us. We just have to make the commitment to be disciplined to learn and improve our knowledge of the crypto space and blockchain industry, which is actually more like digging into a rabbit hole cause the more you know, the more you will realize that you don't know, which will create the desire and devotion in you to keep growing your knowledge base and understanding capacity to earn more income, revenue, and create solutions for others.

There are several ways you can make money, generate revenue, and build wealth with Bitcoin. Generating income with Bitcoin is not difficult; you can make money by Lending, Trading, Buying and Holding, Mining, creating valuable goods & services, and getting payment in Bitcoin for exchange of value. We have several people who have changed their financial fortunes by simply taking advantage of the opportunities that have been made available by Bitcoin and Blockchain Technology in our day and age. They took the bold steps to buy cryptocurrencies at their low rates as investments for the long-term, and when such cryptocurrency project gains more prominence and real-world user cases, their long bought cryptocurrencies in their wallets bring them into abundance. Some of these blockchain tokens and projects could even be for fun, education, entertainment, games, or community service tokens.

For example, Glauber Contessoto took a bold step on Doge Coin, a meme-inspired cryptocurrency that began as a joke. Glauber invested about $250,000 from his personal savings when it was priced at about 4.5 cents in February 2021 during the Bull run market of 2021. About 2 months later, on April 15, 2021, he became a doge coin millionaire.[69] Although He refused to sell and instead chose to keep buying and holding the portfolio of the Doge Coin despites its volatility and ups and downs. This is because even the World's Richest Man,[70] Elon Musk, is a proud supporter and advocate of the meme-themed coin called Doge Coin.[71]

Another amazing story is that of two brothers, James and Tommy, living in Westchester, New York, who became multi-millionaires after buying Shiba Inu with $200 each,[72] and later told their family members about it, who also bought the coin with like $100 each. The entire family's money used in the purchase was $900.[73.] During the bull run market of 2021, they were shocked to see their family's $900 turn into $9 million dollars.[74] This story was investigated and documented by the world's renowned News media outlet, CNN.

There are several other amazing, life-changing stories of how people who have literally nothing are becoming something, entering into financial abundance and wealth by buying, trading, and investing in Cryptocurrencies and Blockchain Technology tokens created to provide solutions to real world problems. When they were just created and newly developed like Solana (SOL), Binance (BNB), Pancake Swap (CAKE), these tokens investment grew as much as 41,798.57% for Solana,[75] 230,184.69% for Binance,[76] 623.50% for Pancake Swap.[77] There are several other tens of credible cryptocurrency projects and blockchain technology software geared towards various sectors with utility, real world user cases, and adoption strategies that have performed and done excellently well like the few ones mentioned above. You need to dig deep in your research and keep your ears on the ground to acquire information and intelligence in the Crypto space that will revolutionize your life and fortunes. Truly, wealth rides on the wings of information and ideas.

One such project that comes to mind recently is the World Coin (WLD), which grew in its valuation and market capitalization to a staggering $20 Billion dollars within hours after it launched in July 2023.[78] A blockchain technology project founded by Sam Altman, an American entrepreneur, investor, programmer, and CEO of OpenAI platform, an American Artificial Intelligence company, creator of Artificial Intelligence products like Chat GPT. The World Coin token is the native token of the Blockchain Technology project created by Sam Altman for Privacy-Preserving Digital Identity by providing its users with verified digital identity.[79]

It's of utmost importance to note that as awesome, amazing, revolutionary, and lifechanging Cryptocurrencies and

Blockchain Technologies can be, it is a very highly volatile market and very risky if in-depth technical knowledge is lacking, mostly unregulated, susceptible to risks of cyber-attacks, loss of wallets password, hacked servers, migrations of projects layers and links, etc. that could cause an individual to loss their funds.

CHAPTER 6
FINANCIAL EDUCATION, INTELLIGENCE, & FREEDOM

There are Billions of people in the world today, and of the 8 billion people we have in the world,[80] only a very tiny, minute, handful fraction are Billionaires. To put it in actual numbers and figures, the total number of wealthy Billionaires in the world today is 2,640, according to Forbes Billionaire's list.[81] Have you ever thought about it? How come that, with all of the wealth, abundance, riches, surplus, and natural resources that are in the world, Why are many people poor? Barely surviving, living from paychecks to paychecks, many in debt, lacking enough resources and money to cater to their personal and family needs and to be a blessing to their community and the world at large?

How come that just 1% of the Richest people own half of the world's wealth, while the poorest half of the world owns 0.75%? [82] Why is it that 81 Billionaires have more wealth than 50% of the world combined?[83] Why do we keep having a sharp simultaneous contrast between extreme Wealth and extreme Poverty in the last 25 years when the world has experienced huge economic numbers?[84] The World Bank estimates that due to the COVID-19 pandemic, the poorest 40% experienced income losses that were double the losses of the richest 20%.[85] Why are poor countries spending 4 times more repaying their debts (often to richer countries and wealthy financial institutions) than on health care and welfare of their citizen?[86]

Also, Food and Energy companies have more than doubled their profits in 2022, yet in stark contrast, the World Food Program estimates that 824 million people go to bed hungry every night in 2022.[87] We can have a lot of reasons and arguments for these solemn answers to the thought-provoking and heart-searching questions above, but at the very center of all. The right and wise answers will be a lack of Financial Education, Financial Intelligence, and Discipline to do that which is right and necessary for Many people for the long-term gain in their health, welfare, resources, and wellbeing. Just as scripture states, "God said, my People are destroyed, impoverished, defeated, brought down and low, for their lack of knowledge."[88]

A lot of people all over the world today are living less than their potential and below their capabilities, with loads of their potentials, talents, and gifts not being used to benefit mankind, humanity, their society, and the world at large, because they are barely surviving, trying to make ends meet, instead of living out their capabilities, gifts, and skills for the world to see and make lasting, valuable impact. Their lack of Financial Education (sound Knowledge) and Financial Intelligence (wisdom and understanding) have cost them their dreams, visions, passions, and fulfillments that they could have attained and achieved if only they give their attention and efforts to gain valuable, financial wisdom and knowledge that would help them to gain Financial Freedom in order to be FREE. For them to do whatever they want to do, go wherever they want to go and spend time with the people they really want to spend their time with.

Most of these Billionaires and wealthy folks that we talked about earlier have created phenomenally successful businesses, created technologies, and innovations that have helped and changed the world in very significant ways. What's their secret to attaining such abundance and freedom? What's their Belief System? What's their Mental Attitude, Character, and Personalities like? What gives them the level of zeal and energy with which they pursue their visions and dreams? What do they know that we don't know? How did they get to where they are today? And how can we embark on the same journey of abundance and freedom? And be sure to arrive where they arrive, too, even if it's in our own little community, society, and country?

It all starts and begins first with Wisdom and Understanding. Just as scripture states, "Wisdom is the principal and most important thing. Therefore, get Wisdom! With everything that you have, Get Understanding also."[89] Wisdom is what gives birth to wealth and abundance. Ideas and information are the tools and instruments used for wealth creation. Without quality information and ideas that help us to create quality goods and services, value creation and innovations, we can't create lasting wealth. Understanding this is very vital, because our minds are the very engine that drives and conceptualizes the entire journey to our financial abundance and freedom. How we think and reason in our minds determines our actions and, therefore, determines the results that we get and have in our lives.

WHAT IS FINANCIAL EDUCATION REALLY?

Financial Education can mean a lot of things to many people. But most times, what we have is often the wrong definition because we've been educated or, better still, indoctrinated wrongly by our teachers, parents, schools, societies, and the financial systems of this world. It's shocking to realize that many of us are not adequately taught about Money in schools and prepared well for life's challenges and difficulties. Sure, we got to learn some math and maybe a few basic skills about how to balance a checkbook, but these concepts are just the tip of the iceberg, and far too many people never really bother to explore the enormous mass of frozen financial education that is under the water for their financial freedom and liberty.

According to a 2019 study of financial literacy by Organization for Economic Co-operation and Development (OECD), over 20% of American teenagers are considered financially illiterate.[90] At best, these teenagers can maybe identify products and terms and make simple decisions regarding everyday spending. This number is much lower in other countries like China and Russia, where only one in 10 teenagers has the same financial illiteracy.

The wealthy are living proof that financial education is one of the most important and vitals skills to have. Without it, we make poor financial decisions and choices in our daily lives. How else are we going to know how to use our Credit Card efficiently? How do we learn to create a budget and implement it? How do we learn to invest in the stock market and cryptocurrencies? How do we plan our retirement? You may have realized just how little you know about finances, and you could even find yourself looking for in the wrong places.

Since our governments and political leaders have failed us when it comes to getting the financial education needed to succeed in life. Maybe it's by design to keep everyone (masses) working for corporations, to collect higher taxes from them than the wealthy, and to keep them living in debt. Maybe they are aware of the facts surrounding our education system but don't know how to change the curriculum accordingly.

Therefore, it behooves us that we take the personal responsibility to handle, train, and develop ourselves on the right financial knowledge and skills needed to get out of the ceaseless, endless, and tiring rat race of life. And if you are a parent already, you must take the parental responsibility to teach and train your children on finances to make them better kids. Their schools and teachers won't do it for you, and they won't do it for them. What do their Teachers and Professors know about Money, Wealth, Abundance, and financial freedom? Yes, you guessed right, little less to nothing, cause they themselves are also in the rat race, struggling, living paycheck to paycheck without having financial freedom.

Financial Education is the body of knowledge that is centered on developing your ability to understand and effectively use various financial skills, which includes personal financial management, investing, risk management, trusts, and legacy, etc. This body of knowledge prepares you and makes you well sophisticated enough to handle money and finance decisions wisely, to frame the course and direction of your life to abundance, wealth, and freedom.

Financial Intelligence is the key to seeing money where nobody else does. True financial freedom is only possible when you have financial intelligence. When your financial intelligence is well enhanced, you'll be able to take advantage of wealth-creating opportunities than the average typical Joe. Financial Intelligence is like the prism of your mind which you use to extract the various kinds of rainbow colors and make better financial decisions than most people because you are seeing things differently and thinking differently from the rest of the world. Financial intelligence helps the workings of your mind to comprehend how money works globally.

We may not be able to capture everything that Financial Education, Financial Intelligence, and Financial Freedom encapsulate in this chapter, but several prominent and well-renowned authors like Robert Kiyosaki have written books on these topics. I'll implore you to get some of these books from any online and physical bookstore and dig deeper into these areas to improve and enhance your mental, financial framework, capacity, and prowess.

For instance, your level of Financial Intelligence will

determine what you will see as risky or not risky? What you'll consider to be an Asset, and what you consider a liability? What you will prioritize between Cash flow and Capital gains when making an investment. What you'll pursue between having Job Security and Financial freedom? What you considered as wealth, and what is truly the measure of wealth. Your level of financial intelligence will determine how you will handle debt. Whether as a tool to move your financial life forward into liberty or as a detonation that blows up your mental health and peace of mind and destroys your finances.

Financial Intelligence also involves the understanding that there are 3 different types of income (or ways that you can make money, that it doesn't have to be through your paid job as an employee only) and the understanding of the impact of these different types of income on your wealth and financial freedom journey. For example, when you make money through a paycheck, you are exchanging your most valuable, precious, limited resources, which is Time for Money. This type of income is called Earned Income, and it is the most taxed among all the 3 types of incomes.

When you make money by buying stock in a corporation at a given price and you are selling the same stock at a higher price in the future. Like if you buy a stock at $20 today, and the price goes up to $50 when you sell the stock, you've made $30 in Capital gains. This type of income is known as Portfolio Income. But if you buy a rental property or a share of a partnership with a business that generates cash for you daily or monthly, this is known as Passive Income. The advantage of Passive Income is that once you have an asset, it provides Cash Flow whether you are working or not. Money keeps coming into your account, and you are free to do other things, like finding more cash-flowing assets. It takes a high Financial Intelligence and Patience to invest successfully for passive income, and these are two things Most people in the world simply don't have.

IS THERE REALLY SUCH A THING AS JOB SECURITY?

The long-aged myth that the only way to be successful financially is by going to school, getting good grades, getting a good paying job with security, and then saving to get a house is no longer valid in our generation and time as we can see unprecedented layoffs and unemployment. Job Security is a nice sentiment from a different generation (the industrial age and early baby boomers). The reality is that in today's economy and financial world being an Employee is the riskiest position of all to be. Don't bank your financial future on working for someone else. Today, many people have gotten good grades, but there are fewer and fewer secure, good paying jobs with benefits like pensions.

Many people need to start "Minding their Own Business," including many unemployed graduates seeking a job where they will mind someone else's business. The allure of what appears to be security is understandable, but as you develop your financial intelligence, you'll see right through the smoke screens that there is no job security that you need to learn to make your own way in the world. To have a secure financial future and freedom in this generation, it is best sought through entrepreneurship and investments and not through employment because, at some point, it dawns on every employee (probably while saving away at their desk well past dinner one evening), that they aren't in charge.

When you work for a company, you are not in the driver's seat of your financial journey. You work the hours they assigned, if you are very hardworking and lucky, you get a raise or promotion when they allow it or decide to. You are stuck with the team they hired, you get a vacation when they approve, and you could be fired or laid off with no notice. This perspective might make you think twice about the so-called "Job Security" you are lucky to have as an Employee. Why would you let a money-hungry, profit-centric company determine your value, worth and your future? Possibly because you've been taught, schooled, and indoctrinated to view the best alternative as risky.

If you look closely at the picture above. You will observe that you have 4 Quadrants.

E (Employee) – as an Employee, you exchange your time and your efforts or income. If you are not working, either because you are sick, had an accident, or got laid off, you are not going to be paid. Your Employer determines what you are paid and what your contribution is worth. Your security is 100% in the hands of your Employer, no matter what you do.

S (Self-Employed) – as a Self-Employed, you work for yourself and may eventually see the result of the time and effort that you put into your work. Flexibility and freedom are still not necessarily attainable here. Whereas as an

Employee, you "have" a job, as a Self-Employed, you simply "own" a job.

B (Business Owner) – as a Business Owner, you will have a Business that generates passive income from creating goods and services, valuable impact, and solutions that people need centered around your areas of visions, gifts, talents, potentials, and passion. You will see the direct result of your time and effort, and your income doesn't really rely on your active work. Here, you have the ability to determine the fate of your future; you may even have people working hard for you to generate income through Daily Cash Flow from your Business Systems.

I (Investor) – as an Investor, the only thing working here is your Money, that you have rightfully and wisely deployed into strategic investments like Bitcoin, Oil & Gas, Energy, NASDAQ, etc. You on a golf course or vacation.

Those on the left side of the Quadrant, Employees, and Self-Employed, are the ones at the most risk because they have no control and lose the most money they make to taxes and inflation. Those on the right, Business Owners and Investors, even though they have traditionally been viewed as the riskiest, are actually the most secure because they have control to determine what happens directly to their income and can use taxes and inflation to their advantage. Here is the hard truth, security is a myth. The trajectory for Employee's income is not good, and when there is a bad economic time, it is the employees who lose their jobs, not the Business Owners.

Learn something new and take on this brave new world. Don't hide from it, don't cringe in fear, and don't cower into your false security. It's also risky for the Self-Employed; if they get sick or injured, their income is directly impacted. The more fatigue a person endures, the less secure they become and the risk of having an accident also goes up. As the march of technology like automation continues at an ever-increasing pace, employees and the self-employed have to constantly be trained to keep up and stay relevant in the job market. Look at it this way, if you are going to reeducate anyway, why not spend some time educating yourself on the skills needed to become a Business Owner or Investor on the right side of the Cashflow Quadrant?

WHAT'S THE SECURED PATH THAT LEADS TO FREEDOM?

The Irony is that on the right side of the quadrant, the one viewed by most people as most risky is actually the path that is most secure and leads to Financial Freedom, wealth, and abundance. For example, if you have a secure Business system that produces more and more money with less and less work, then you really don't need a job to worry about losing your job. To make more money and increase your income, you just simply expand your business system and hire more people; that gives you the opportunity to expand your means and revenue so that you enjoy all that life has to offer.

Also, people who are high-level Investors aren't concerned about market volatility, the going up and down of price values of their stocks and cryptocurrencies because their knowledge and financial intelligence allows them to make money in either situation. Even if there is a market crash for the foreseeable future, which isn't entirely unlikely. Many people who are not well trained with in-depth knowledge of how the stocks and crypto market work will panic and loose the money they had for retirement plans. If that happens in their old age, instead of retiring, they'll have to work for as long as they can. How is that Security? Professional and Highly Sophisticated Investors are people who risk little of their own money and yet still make the highest returns. The people who know little about investing take risks and earn the least return.

You can create your own security, and with self-employment, you can diversify your client base in a way that provides the job security you need to sleep well each night. If you happen to lose a client, you still have others who will keep the money rolling in while you look for a replacement. Entrepreneurship offers a virtually unlimited income potential because they can drum up more business if they need more money. You also set your own prices, which means you can charge what your time and expertise are worth in the market. Once your business is booming and doing excellently well, you can cherry-pick which clients you want to work with and avoid the ones who are difficult or who don't pay you on time. You will never again be in a position where you'll have to endure something that frustrates you or threatens your livelihood because you control the direction and wheel of your own business. This is the true real job security.

Your financial security and financial freedom are all about you; you will need to take the personal responsibility to learn, unlearn, and relearn new methodologies and approaches of how to move from the left side of the Quadrant to the right side of the quadrant. Today is a good day to start. I recommend that you buy and study books on business development, investing, personal finance, budgeting & debt management, and get Robert Kiyosaki's book titled, "Rich Dad Cashflow Quadrant: Guide to Financial Freedom." The more you develop, train, and equip yourself with the right skills, mindsets, beliefs, mental attitude, networks, relationships, opportunities, and effective execution of your plans, goals, ideas, and visions, the better and faster you get on your journey to financial freedom, abundance, impact, and fulfillment.

CHAPTER 7
BITCOIN & BLOCKCHAIN TECHNOLOGY SOLVES GOVERNMENT PROBLEMS

Although, most governments are strong antagonists of Bitcoin and Blockchain Technology because Bitcoin and Blockchain Technology are highly decentralized, without the need for any interference of third parties and intermediaries, and they can't control it, print more of it, regulate its monetary policy, or do anything to control its freedom and sovereignty. Conventional Currencies like Dollars, Yen, Euros, Pounds, etc., are entirely centralized. The government of its country has the power to control it, and the government can alter its financial policy to run the economy and control how the public spends the money and how their wealth is being used and valued. The Government can also easily track and monitor fraudulent, criminal activities, terrorism, and other financial vices that tend to destroy the lives and property of its citizens.

The conventional use of fiat currencies gives Governments the power to influence and control their economy. However, with the advent of Bitcoin and Blockchain Technology, the Governments and Central Banks have lost control of the Decentralized currency, and this is one of their biggest fears and worries. But instead of being so concerned and worried about losing control and the threats of freedom that Bitcoin and Blockchain Technology give to people. They should look at the huge, enormous benefits, value addition and problems that Bitcoin helps them to solve. One of the highest prices for Freedom is Responsibility. The more people are able to have their financial freedom, the more responsibility they can take for themselves and their families.

Even though Bitcoin and Blockchain Technology are still a very young, volatile cryptocurrency that has only been available for a decade, fiat currency has been around for much longer, and its price value is relatively stable, even though we can't say the same for its purchasing power. Most Governments have not taken enough time to carry out due diligent, thorough, and holistic research on Bitcoin, its technology, software, protocols, security, energy, and uses. One of the greatest fears of mankind is the fear of the unknown. We are hardly afraid or fearful of that which we have adequate, correct, and comprehensive knowledge about, this is true for every field and in every human endeavor, be it in medicine, science, art, aeronautics, space research, etc. Countries like El Salvador have declared Bitcoin as a legal tender because they've done their thorough research and this singular chess move has helped to revolutionize the country's government bonds, tourism, security, and economy.[91] Whereas some countries still do not want to do anything with the decentralized currency because of fear, ignorance, greed or all the above.

The Governments will be shocked and amazed at the facts they will discover; they will find out how secure and impregnable to attacks and fraudulent manipulations the multi-layered Bitcoin network's security, the transaction hashing, mining, blocks of confirmations, and game theory all work together to make the Bitcoin's blockchain impenetrable.[92] Since the first transaction block in 2009, the network has NEVER been shut down, and no Bitcoin has ever been stolen.[93] Every transaction on the Bitcoin Blockchain is verified by multiple nodes on the network, making it impossible to alter data fraudulently. It's, therefore, an incredibly secure way to store data, transfer value, and carry out transactions without breach of trust by third-party intermediaries, contracts, documents, and agreements.

This is one of the platforms that the committee of nations and global powers need amongst themselves, as they do not truly and really trust each other, even as we've seen in the recent geopolitical wars, economic conflicts, and trade relations issues arising from the Russia-Ukraine war. Many nations have been experiencing currency wars over the years due to the manipulation and devaluation of the country's currency by itself or by another bigger entity.

ECONOMIC AND CURRENCY WARS

Currency War is simply the manipulation of currency. Currency manipulation happens when a government or central bank introduces monetary policy or financial measures with the purpose and intent of weakening its own currency or that of another country. A Currency war can break out after a country deliberately devalues its own currency and prompts another country to do the same; this is known as Competitive Devaluation. Countries purposely cause their currencies to depreciate in the hope that it can invigorate economic growth and give them an edge over other nations. Currency Wars are all about tit for tat; when a country has devalued its currency, then others regard it as an act of economic war and respond in kind. A country only devalues its currency out of self-interest and at the expense of other countries, which in turn do not like to feel as if they are losing out or being taken advantage of by another country's monetary policy.

It is important to note that a country can aim to weaken its own currency without igniting a currency war, but if another country responds by devaluing its own currency, then a war can break out nonetheless. There are good benefits to having a strong currency. It can help to reduce the price of imports and improve the standard of living of its citizens, who enjoy a greater purchasing power when buying goods from around the world. It can also help to keep inflation in check and encourage companies to become more competitive and efficient.

THE EFFECTS OF A WEAKER CURRENCY

Every action and decision has its corresponding conse-quences and effects when a country's currency is being deval-ued. It put some economic constraint on the people and citizens of the country, even though the government can be using it as a measure to save its crumbling economy. When a country depreciates its currency value, it becomes more expensive to produce goods and services in the country as the price and demand for production goes up. Although this can help to increase the country's exports as their goods and services are cheaper and more affordable to other countries with a currency that has stronger value and high purchasing power.

A country with a weaker currency also means that importing goods into the country becomes very expensive, people won't be able to easily afford and import foreign goods because of their weak currency. However, if the country is very creative and resourceful, citizens can be encouraged to purchase locally-made or home-based products as alternatives. This can help to increase demand for the country's home-made products. This will invariably boost the country's exports while discouraging the imports of foreign goods and services, which can have a dramatic effect on the country's terms of trade. Exporting more and importing less will mean a country's trade deficit (when import is more than export) will reduce. And if a country is already in a trade surplus (when it exports more than it imports), then it will grow.

A weaker currency can help the government of a country to attract more foreign investors into the country as Assets, housing, and stocks become cheaper for overseas investors as they can buy more assets with their money with a stronger currency, to the detriment of the nation's citizens. Also, a country can devalue its currency as a measure to manage its debt because devaluing its currency also effectively devalues any outstanding loans denominated in that currency. The Lender Country and Government tend to lose out when the currency is weakened, as the amount, they will receive back from the borrower will ultimately be worth less than what it was when the loan was issued. This is good news for the Borrowing Country and Government as it can make repayments more manageable and reduce the overall amount that needs to be paid back, but this is also at the detriment of its people and citizens, as they lose their money, wealth, and assets to devaluation.

There is always a risk in the devaluation of a country's currency, which is why the international community will often disagree with a country's plan to devalue its currency. And as part of sanction measures to be meted out to a country for its chargeable or treasonable offense, the international community can decide to give sanctions that will cripple the economy of the county and devalue its currency, thereby making the harsh effect of the devaluation to be felt by all its citizens and people. If the Country decides to retaliate back by doing the same, and then vice versa, then this leads to a full-blow currency war. An example of this can be seen in the ongoing Russia-Ukraine geopolitical war, which has involved the West, EU, China, and even the forming of a new global alliance called the BRICS+ (Brazil, Russia, India, China, India, South Africa, et al.) intended to de-dollarized the US Dollars as the world's currency reserve.[94] The Russian ruble has lost 25% of its value since the beginning of the year 2023,[95] and is hitting its lowest level in 17 months since the war began, and worth less than a cent.[96]

It is unsurprising that more countries are considering the weaponization of currencies in today's world, where protectionism is rising, borders are being erected, globalization is being slowly eroded by state governments, and economic growth is slow and stagnating. Many economists regard currency wars as counter-intuitive because they can spur on inflation and raise the cost of living for citizens. The Central Bank of a country is usually the one in charge of the country's monetary policy; they are the ones who design and architect any plan to devalue a currency. Some countries like China peg their currency to another currency (Yuan to Dollar). If China wants to devalue the Yuan, then it simply has to adjust the peg to which the exchange rate is fixed.

THE ONGOING CURRENCY WAR BETWEEN CHINA – USA, AND OTHER GLOBAL POWERS.

The two countries in the world with the strongest economies are the USA and China, with a GDP (Gross Domestic Product) of 26.85 trillion dollars and 19.37 trillion dollars, respectively, with Japan, Germany, and India sitting together with them in the top 5 positions.[97] They all contribute to almost half of the world's global economy [98] The ripple effect of this is that when anything happens to their economy, it affects every nation of the world. In recent years, the United States of America and China have been in a trade war, which was full-blown to media during President Donald Trump's Administration in 2018.[99] The term currency war was used by Brazil's finance minister Gudio Mantega in September 2010 to describe the economic tussle between the leading world powers, when He argued that USA, China, and others had sparked a race to devalue their currencies to gain a competitive edge and that this was causing the currencies of Brazil and other emerging economies to rise and hurting economic growth.[100]

China, which pegged the Yuan to the dollar in 2007, had been spending billions of dollars to keep its currency weak against that of the US. Japan has done the same by selling Yen and buying dollars. Numerous countries, including Switzerland and Israel, have also tried to lower the value of their currencies. This slowly strengthened the Dollar, which in the past would have suited the US and its policy to have a stronger currency, Dollar. However, over time the USA now feels other countries have purposely kept the value of their currencies low relative to the dollar in order to secure large trade surpluses and an advantage over US companies. The growing tensions between the US and China have caused the US to start shifting away from its strong currency policies, and now it's aiming to weaken the dollar to make US manufacturers and exporters more competitive.

As far as the United States government is concerned, the reason the US has such a large trade deficit compared to China is that it has purposely kept the value of the Yuan low for decades, and for this to change, the Dollar must weaken, and the Yuan must strengthen. The current fears and worries for governments, political leaders, and economists surrounding currency wars have emerged after China refused to intervene to stop the Yuan from devaluing further against the dollar. It has traditionally ensured that one Dollar would equal no more than six Yuan, but recently let that slip to over seven Yuan to prompt fear that China is manipulating its currency.[101] This is significant because it comes at a time when trade tensions between the two countries are already high, demonstrating that countries devalue their currencies as part of a wider strategy involving tariffs, capital controls, and other trade policies.

This ongoing economic war between the USA and China

has further escalated recently after China showed its support and alliance for Russia,[102] despite all the sanctions imposed on Russia by the USA, United Kingdom, and European Union for its invasion of Ukraine in February 2022.[103] This has further aggravated after China and Russia teamed up with other countries to form the BRICS alliance with the aim of dethroning the US Dollar because it was weaponized as part of the sanction measures mete out to Russia for its invasion to Ukraine. The Western Governments (USA, UK, and EU) froze Russia's central banks' foreign currency reserve held within its jurisdiction, a currency war chest of $600 billion dollars.[104]

This was unprecedented in the history of government policies, regulations, economy, and interrelationships. This move by the United States of America, the United Kingdom, and the European Union led to a stronger partnership of Russia and China with other countries in the BRICS alliance to look for another alternative currency for their foreign reserve and trade settlements to avoid being taken down economically or punished by the same measures.[105]

BITCOIN & BLOCKCHAIN TECHNOLOGY COMING TO THE RESCUE?

The World's global economic scale is undergoing a major paradigm shift and changing very fast right now, with so much distrust among political and world leaders, misappropriation of government funds, and abuse of power. All these challenges can be tackled and solved if the governments of the nations are willing to pay the price for the adoption of Bitcoin and Blockchain. The BRICS committee is already weighing this option as part of their alternatives from the hegemony of the dollar and fiat currency.[106] Major Banks across the world are failing and declaring bankruptcy, Saudi Arabia and Iran are negotiating historic and many countries are beginning to have plans to deviate from the US Dollar as the world reserve currency, with considerations on United States enormous debts.[107]

Bitcoin's underlying blockchain technology provides a promising framework for a more streamlined and efficient financial system that helps to tackle all the bottlenecks and bureaucracy in the interdependency of nations, especially global powers. The adoption of Bitcoin's blockchain technology in the financial architecture of BRICS countries could enhance transparency, security, and efficiency in various financial transactions, including cross-border payments and remittances. Bitcoin's decentralized nature and limited supply also help to offer economic stability and greatly reduce the issue of currency devaluation by external economic factors by any government central bank's monetary policy.

For this global and national adoption to be seamless, a regulatory landscape for various countries will need to be in place to ensure identity compliance, consumer protection, and security for users. Proactive measures to address the price volatility would also be in place for the value of other goods & services. A robust digital infrastructure that includes secure wallets, exchanges, and payment gateways that would support effortless and seamless Bitcoin transactions for the ordinary average people. General education and training of people of bitcoin's use, once all these adoption measures have been put in place by the governments, their economy, and citizens will experience radical growth, welfare, and national transformation.

CHAPTER 8

THEY IGNORE YOU, THEN THEY JOIN YOU? CBDCS AND GLOBAL ASSETS MANAGERS

The wise quote of the old India sage, Mahatma Gandhi, says that, "First they ignore you, then they laugh at you, then they fight you, then you win." This can be said about Bitcoin and Blockchain Technology, first, it was ignored by the world's governments and people, then they laughed at it and called it several names like a fad, a bubble, etc. Then, with time, they fought it with their laws, policies, and regulations to ban its operations. But Bitcoin and its Blockchain Technology have refused to die, rather, it keeps evolving and growing at a faster adoption rate than even the Internet.[108] New innovations are often hard to digest for humanity such is the case of Cryptocurrency. We criticize, attack, and reject things that we don't understand too soon, but as the Cryptocurrency space continues to gain more dominance with a market valuation of over $1 Trillion dollars,[109] many governments, institutional investors, and global assets managers are beginning to make a move for its use, application, and adoption.

GOVERNMENT'S ADOPTION OF BLOCKCHAIN FOR CBDCS

Many Countries are now adopting blockchain technology to develop their own CBDCs, and some have implemented theirs as many more are researching ways to transition to Digital Currency. What are CBDCs? It's important to understand what they are and what they mean to the financial system of their respective country. CBDCs are a form of digital currency issued by a country's central bank and ruling government; they are like cryptocurrencies, except that their value is fixed by the central bank and equivalent to the country's fiat currency. Fiat Money is a government-issued currency that has no backing from a physical commodity like gold or silver. It is considered as a legal tender that can be used to exchange for goods and services.

Traditionally, Fiat money came as banknotes and coins, but the advent of blockchain technology has allowed and forced governments and financial institutions to supplement physical fiat money with a credit-based model that records balances and transactions globally. Physical currency is still widely used, exchanged, and accepted; however, some developed countries have experienced a drop in its use, and this trend accelerated during the COVID-19 pandemic. The advent and evolution of cryptocurrency and blockchain technology have created further interest in cashless and digital currencies.

In the U.S and many other countries, many people don't have access to financial services; they are called the "Unbanked." in the U.S alone, 5% of adults did not have a bank account in 2020, and these numbers are larger in Africa and Asia, some as high as 40%.[110] Additional 13% of U.S adults who had bank accounts instead used costly alternatives like money orders, payday loans, and check cashing services. The main goal of CBDCs is to provide businesses and consumers with privacy, transferability, convenience, accessibility, and financial security. CBDCs could also help governments and Banks to reduce the cost of maintenance that a complex financial system requires, reduce cross-border transaction costs, and provide those who currently use alternative money-transfer methods with lower cost options.

Governments said that CBDCs would help to reduce the risks associated with using digital currencies, or cryptocurrencies, in their current form. Cryptocurrencies are highly volatile, with their value constantly fluctuating. This volatility could cause severe financial stress in many households and affect the overall stability of an economy. Governments believe that they can monitor and track fraudulent transactions, organized crime, and terrorism financing with the use of their CBDCs because they can decipher and unravel the individuals and organizations carrying out such activities, which is very hard and difficult when compared to Cryptocurrencies that have anonymous identity. CBDCs, backed by a government and controlled by a central bank, would give households, consumers, and businesses a secure means of exchanging digital currency.

However there are some major concerns and issues being raised with respect to Governments issuing and creating CBDCs backed by their current financial fiat systems. Some of these concerns, issues, and risks have been debated, argued, and talked about in various parliament houses, senate houses, media houses, and public spaces. We will delve into a few of the concerns and risks of CBDCs to the average general citizen of any country or government that issues a CBDCs.

Just like the paper fiat currency (dollar, yen, euros, naira, etc.), a central bank digital currency known as CBDCs would be under the liability of the federal reserve or the central banking system of the country, and unlike paper fiat currency, CBDCs will not offer the privacy protection, personal data security, and finality that paper fiat (cash) provides. The direct, digital liability makes CBDCs a radical departure from the digital money that millions of people in the world are using already in the world today, in the forms of mobile banking, internet banking, digital money payments, card payments and, point of sales transactions, etc.

CBDCs may not necessarily offer unique benefits to the citizens of a country compared to the already existing digital money and payment technologies, it would sure make it faster, more efficient to use, and scalable to the unreached and unbanked people in the world, but it poses serious risks to the very little or nothing privacy protection that remains for the average individual and citizen of a country whose central banking system is using CBDCs. We don't know who is using a 100 Dollar bill today, and we don't know who is using a 1,000 Peso bill or Naira bill today. The key difference with the CBDCs is that the Central Bank of the country will have absolute control over the rules and regulations that will determine the use of expression of that Central Bank's liability, and we will have the technology to enforce that.

Simply put, a CBDCs would most likely be the single largest assault to financial privacy since the creation of the Bank Secrecy Act and the establishment of the third-party doctrine. The threat to freedom that a CBDCs could pose is closely related to its threat of privacy. With so much data in hand, a CBDCs would provide any Government and the Central Banking system of any country that issues it countless opportunities to control citizen's financial activity.

FREEZING AND SEIZING OF ASSETS

Governments have long discovered and recognized that freezing or seizing someone's financial resources is one of the most effective ways to lock them out of society. A CBDCs will make that easier and faster for governments by establishing a direct line between the governments and the citizens through the use of the Central Bank Digital Currencies.

NEGATIVE INTEREST RATES

While most interest rates are typically thought of to be in positive terms, a CBDCs could allow policy makers and governments to set a negative rate. A negative interest rate would spur people to borrow more money, spend more on the economy, and save less, as interest rates are unimaginably zero or nothing, and in the long run, make people lose their money or wealth.

PROGRAMMABLE SPENDING

The use of CBDCs by governments and their programmable characteristics could be used by governments to prohibit people from buying certain goods and services, with a limit on how much they can purchase or spend to buy something. For example, policymakers and governments could try to curb how much is spent on foreign imported goods and people with past records of offenses. By programming a CBDCs, people's money can be controlled and precisely targeted for what people can own and what they can do with their money.

A CBDCs can undermine both the foundation and future of financial markets by reducing Credit availability, disintermediating Banks, and challenging the rise of Cryptocurrency. It could be used as one of the tools by Governments to fight and undermine the advantages and freedom that Bitcoin and Blockchain Technology made available for the average individual of any country in this world.

CENTRALIZATION & DATA SECURITY

Another concern with CBDCs is the central control and storage of information. If there is an IRS breach or cyber-attack, this puts millions of citizens of the country at risk. Whereas a breach of a private financial institution or a bank would only put very few citizens of the bank at risk leaving customers from other banks free from risk. Unlike a rigorous cyber-attack on the Bitcoin networks and other Decentralized Blockchain networks, which are very difficult and nearly impossible to be breached due to their decentralized networks, the CBDCs networks of governments are prone to cyber-attacks and can be easily susceptible to the attacks and be breached because their networks are centralized to one central authority, the Central Banking system of the country.

Although the Governments of many countries are trying to leverage on the blockchain technology and trying to adopt its use for the creation of their own Central Bank Digital Currencies, CBDCs do not want to give out the control, freedom, power, and privacy that the very idea for the creation of Blockchain technology and Bitcoin was birthed on. The Governments of a nation are often controlled by only a very few elites, while millions of the country's citizens suffer and wallow in poverty, economic crisis, poor government policies, infrastructure, healthcare, jobs, financial mobility, and freedom.

There are other better ways that governments can use Blockchain technology to develop their economic growth and help their citizens, but the issuing of a Central Bank Digital Currency that is backed by a government threatens the financial privacy and freedom of its citizens and undermines the financial banking system and cryptocurrency industry. Policymakers and senators, in their congress meetings and debates, should strive to establish and consider these various perspectives and angles on making the decision of whether their country should issue a CBDCs, a digital national currency. It is due to these fundamental threats that the policymakers and governors in some states and countries are pushing back the CDBCs.

For instance, the Federal Reserve Chairman of the United States, Jerome Powell, once said that "We would not want a world in which the Governments sees in real time, every money transfer that anyone makes with a CBDC."[111] In order words, those calling for the rollout of CBDCs are naïve to believe that this can be done without establishing a centralized surveillance system for all financial transactions. The world already has plenty of digital currency, and a CBDCs is not just a paper currency fiat in a digital form. Its adoption would have very serious consequences on the U.S. financial system and economy. Several Senators, House of Representatives, Policymakers, Human Rights leaders, Financial Industry leaders like Senator Ted Cruz, Representative Tom Emmer, Federal Reserve Governor Christopher Waller, Joseph Wang, Rob Morgan, Madison Rose, and Alex Gladstein have all spoken in respect to this.[112] Even Ron DeSantis, the Governor of Florida and presidential candidate signed a bill to prohibit the use of CBDCs within his state and promises to do the same if elected the President of the United States of America.[113]

GLOBAL ASSETS MANAGERS AND BITCOIN

The attention of the world's top global assets managers has been drawn towards Bitcoin and the blockchain technology industry in recent years as a result of its unique, special qualities as a world-renowned digital currency, a security, a store of value and a medium of exchange and for its performance as a global asset that is in constant demand all over the world. Top Global Assets Managers like Goldman Sachs, Blackrock,

Morgan Stanley, Fidelity, Vanguard Group, Charles Schwab, BNY Mellon, and others that handle and manage trillions of the world's global assets are now looking into Bitcoin and other blockchain technologies like Ethereum as an asset they must have in their books. As of today, Bitcoin is still the world's best, most performing asset in the last 10 years when compared to 17 other traditional top-performing assets like Gold, Silver, Commodities, US stocks, Government Bonds, Real Estate (REITs), Mutual Funds, Cash, NASDAQ, SP500, Treasury Bills, etc. despite its volatility.[114]

During the Bitcoin's bull run of 2021, it was the best-performing asset in the world as it hit its all-time high of $69,000 per unit,[115] this historic feat made the world's global assets managers who have, at one point or another, castigated and made bad public judgments about Bitcoin and the Blockchain Industry to put in the research work, study and close monitoring of the digital asset. Between 2011 and 2021, the data examined showed that Bitcoin's cumulative gain in the last 10 years has exceeded 20,000,000%. This has far outpaced the gains and performance of the U.S. large caps and NASDAQ 100, which records 3,282% and 541%, respectively. Bitcoin returned an average of 230% annually within this period; this is 10 times the performance of NASDAQ 100, which is the second-best performing asset of the decade. U.S. large caps annualized returns of 14%, and Gold recorded an annualized return of 1.5%. Even though Bitcoin is a very volatile asset, there is no denying that it is an asset class that needs to be bought, kept, and held as an investment instrument and wealth management.

The realization of these facts is one of the major reasons why these top global asset managers, the biggest banks in Europe and America, hedge funds, and family offices are striving and diving into the large, deep blue ocean of Bitcoin and Blockchain Technology. As they could see that it is an idea and technology that is not going anywhere and is not going to die, just like the advent of internet, web, emails, instant messaging, and the real-time sharing of data and information all over the world are now transforming into real-time sharing of value and transfer of wealth all over the world.

Many Investors and Asset Managers are now considering having some of their portfolios in Bitcoin and other top Blockchain Technology assets. They might own a lot of stocks of several top-performing companies like Coca-Cola, Amazon, Apple, Tesla, Netflix, Google, Microsoft, etc., which is more like owning a fractional ownership interest in the business or company. Some of them are even invested heavily in Governments Bons, Treasury Bills, Securities and Real Estate, Gold, Silver, Precious Gems, etc., but are now looking into moving some part of their entire asset allocation into Bitcoin.

In recent months, several top Global Assets Management firms in the world are now submitting their application for a Bitcoin ETF (Exchange Traded Fund) to the United Sates of America Securities and Exchange Commission called SEC. With the likes of Blackrock, which is the world's largest asset management firm, Grayscale, Fidelity, Franklin Templeton, Ark Investments, Valkyrie, and many other Wall Street insiders submitting their applications for a spot Bitcoin ETF.[116] Of which, according to Forbes, over the last 10 years, the SEC has consistently shut down every application submitted for Bitcoin ETF, but now they can't ignore again.[117]

Blackrock intends to address the fears of the U.S. government's SEC for them to get their approval for Bitcoin's ETF, because many of their client and institutional investors are making a huge demand for Bitcoin as stated by Blackrock's CEO Larry Fink.[118] Larry Fink, the CEO of the $10 Trillion Dollars asset management firm, rightly stated that the approval of the Bitcoin ETF (Exchange-Traded Funds) by the U.S SEC would greatly help to democratize the digital asset among their clients, just as it did with Gold for their Gold Investors, who have been monitoring Bitcoin's performance in the last 5 years.[119]

Many financial industry leaders, asset managers, market analysts, and economists believe strongly that sooner than later, the U.S. SEC will approve the Bitcoin Exchange-Traded Fund, as its an idea whose time has come. And this approval will change the dynamics of asset management and lead to wealth creation & preservation for many people in the world. As they take advantage of the inflow of capital, assets, unique characteristics, edge, and advantage that Bitcoin and Blockchain Technology's ecosystem provides for the average individual against inflation and devaluation risk, economic and geopolitical risk.

CHAPTER 9

RISK AND CHALLENGES OF BITCOIN & BLOCKCHAIN TECHNOLOGY

B itcoin can be likened to the proverbial cat with nine lives for its remarkable immunity to damage, durability, and the ability to survive a lot of attacks, damages, negative press, media, governments ban, restrictions, bad players, and fraudulent financial actors, market volatility, circumstances and situations over the years since its inception in 2009. Through it all, Bitcoin and the Blockchain Technology have survived and weathered the storms, and it's still holding its heads-up high, thriving, and tearing off from its path every opposition and obstacle, blazing the trail and setting the standards for other digital currency, assets and store of value to follow, learn from, and adopt its strategy. With a unit price of each piece of Bitcoin now valued at over $26,500 from what was barely less than a $1,[120] and a market valuation of an entire Blockchain industry valued at $1 Trillion dollars during a bear market,[121] that has seen most digital currency assets depleted by an average of over 70% since the peak of the last bull run in 2022.[122]

Thereby leading to the loss of over $2 Trillion from the crypto blockchain industry since its all-time high during the bull market of 2021.[123] This loss and depletion of value in the Crypto Blockchain industry is not something uncommon. It is often called the "Crypto Winter" cycle, just like every cycle, there would be peaks and lows. There are several factors that cause or drive these cycles, which cause the risk of loss and depreciation of value of Bitcoin and other Blockchain Technologies. We are going to talk about the various risks and challenges of buying, holding, and keeping Bitcoin and other prominent cryptocurrencies.

The Blockchain Technology has raised eyebrows among governments, industry stakeholders, banking sector, asset managers, and individual investors for some of its risks and challenges over the years, despite its astronomical rise since its inception and has taken the world by a storm. Some of the risks and challenges that Bitcoin and its Blockchain Technology are facing are based on ethical, social, technological, and political issues.

VOLATILITY

The risk involves high volatility; Bitcoin has been a very highly volatile asset since its creation. The price and value fluctuate at a very fast rate based on several factors like the law of supply and demand, mining rate, government policies and rules, good or bad media projections in the crypto space, and many more. These factors influence the price and value, and it is of high importance to know that money can be lost during an extremely downward market trend, although in the long run of years, the value can be recovered during an upward market trend, but this is not true for every Blockchain Cryptocurrency. Especially Digital currencies that do not have valuable real-world user cases and utility, poor leadership and management team, misappropriation of customers' funds, and fraudulent practices.

CYBERTHREATS AND ATTACKS

Heavy Cyberthreat and attacks are also some of the risks associated with Blockchain Technologies. Even though several mechanisms and protocols exist to make Bitcoin almost impossible to be breached, hacked, or stolen, some blockchain technologies that do not have such strong blockchain technologies are prone to cyber-attacks that lead to the loss of people's funds. This is often common, especially around new blockchain technology platforms and exchanges and, thereby causing loss of money due to the hacks despite the presence of a smart wallet. For example, in March 2022, the Ronin network used by Axie Infinity blockchain gaming platform was breached by hackers, and the hackers made off with around $625 million worth of Ethereum and USDC stablecoin,[124] thereby causing a loss for people and investors. This is the largest cryptocurrency hack to date,[125] there are several others, like Poly Network in 2021, that hackers made off with $600 million dollars; Coin Check Exchange in 2018 that, hackers made off with $534 million dollars; Mt Gox. Exchange in between 2011 to 2014, lost over 850,000 Bitcoins worth around $470 million dollars at that time due to hacking. In September 2020, KuCoin Exchange network was breached, and the hackers made off with $281 million dollars.[126]

Users should always use cold wallets, which are offline and more secure, to store large amounts of cryptocurrencies. Users should always choose reputable and regulated Exchanges that have adequate security and insurance policies. Cryptocurrencies are an exciting and innovative technology that offers many benefits and opportunities for people all over the world. However, they come with risks and challenges that require vigilance and responsibility. Hackers are constantly looking for ways to exploit vulnerabilities and weaknesses in the Blockchain technology industry. You should always be prepared for the worst-case scenarios. Also, by learning from the past hacks and following best practices, you can protect your digital assets and blockchain technology products while enjoying the Blockchain revolution.

REGULATION AND POLICIES

The lack of regulations and policies that guide and monitor the operation, management and use of funds by blockchain technology firms and Exchanges. This is causing a lot of problems because some fraudulent people do create smart contracts, products, and fake investments, and they run off with people's money. Poor management and handling of users' funds and digital assets by the executives of the blockchain technology firms and Exchanges can also lead to loss of wealth, and this is why many top crypto players in the blockchain industry are calling for Crypto regulation.

TAX PAYMENTS

Many governments are seeking ways to be able to tax people on the gains and profits made on their digital assets and blockchain technology products as they are considered as security or digital property and therefore subjected to Capital gains. When people buy Bitcoin or any digital asset at a low price and sell at a high price, it's expected that tax should be paid. Also, when these digital assets are used to purchase goods and services, the government expects that fees and charges should be paid, but the framework for this is not fully in place in many countries. This is surely one of the reasons why some governments have not adopted its uses.

MAINSTREAM ADOPTION

Since its creation in 2009, it has become easier to buy, sell, and use Bitcoin and other blockchain technology products with their digital assets, but there are still a whole lot of people who have not recognized and taken advantage of the Bitcoin revolution. As of today, September 2023, it is estimated that a very few 420 million people in the world are using Cryptocurrencies out of the 8 billion people we have in the world.[127] This means that there is still tremendous room for growth and adoption in the use of Bitcoin and Blockchain technology, and the less mainstream adoption of Bitcoin as a means of exchange and various Blockchain Technology products for their various real-world uses and problem-solving, the less the growth and advancement of the technology and industry.

Cryptocurrency offers the potential for substantial profits, but it also comes with volatility, risks, and challenges. As the Crypto industry continues to evolve, regulations and government involvement are expected to increase as these will lead to more mainstream adoption due to the confidence and security that is provided by regulatory bodies.

SCALABILITY AND NEW COMPETITIVE TECHNOLOGY

The design, mechanism, and protocols built into the Bitcoin technology limit the amount of information that can be contained in each block to 1 megabyte of data. This programming allows the network capacity of three transactions per second. As more and more transactions are executed, the more difficult the network will face to keep up the records, resulting in delays in processing transactions. This issue is addressed by other Blockchain technologies like Ethereum, which can process 15-20 transactions per second, and other competitive Blockchain technology, like Solana, which can process 50,000 transactions per second. The Blockchain technology industry is still a new technology in its infancy and early stages. These technologies are developing better, faster, and more efficient means of exchange of value and problem-solving techniques every day, making the market and industry to keep evolving. The future may still be unclear for some blockchain products, as they could be displaced by better and more advanced technology.

BAD PRESS AND MEDIA FOR CRIMINAL USE

In its early stages, Bitcoin is well known on the dark Web for money laundering and the purchase of illegal items, drugs, and weapons, because of its anonymous payment features. The Silk Road case is a classic example of this. The online black market founded by Ross Ulbricht, who is now serving a life sentence in prison, served as a platform that ran between 2011-2013 and allowed the use of Bitcoin for anonymous transactions before it was eventually shut down by the FBI in 2013. When the FBI shut down the website, they seized over 144,000 Bitcoins and arrested the founder who has made about $80 million dollars in commissions for transactions carried out on the platform.[128] Also, with the rise in the use of Bitcoin and Blockchain Technologies, many scammers and fraudulent people have created fake Exchanges to steal people's money. Several law-abiding citizens have been warned to avoid and stay away from any blockchain products or digital assets due to the bad reputation and perception created by these fraudulent people who lack integrity.

UNCERTAINTY OF GOVERNMENT POLICIES

Even though Bitcoin and Blockchain Technologies products have emerged as new modes of payment, only a few institutions, countries and governments have officially recognized it as an authorized mode of transaction as a Legal Tender and viable currency. The lack of clear and uniform governmental regulations both within and across countries, European Unions, the United Arab Emirates, and the USA creates an air of uncertainty for long-term investors. For instance, in the U.S., it is still unclear when a cryptocurrency or blockchain technology product falls under the regulatory framework of a security that is subject to the Securities and Exchange Commission regulations and when it is deemed to be an asset or commodity like Bitcoin and Ethereum have claimed. Also, in some countries, Cryptocurrencies and Blockchain technology products are facing outright prohibition and ban. China's abrupt banning of all cryptocurrency trading and mining in 2021 is a vivid example, but it was not the only country that did that. Several countries like Algeria, Nepal, Bolivia, Morocco, Egypt, and Bangladesh.[129]

Regulators and policymakers have also been concerned with the notable and repeated breakdown in the infrastructure supporting cryptocurrency mining and trading, another area where there is significant regulatory uncertainty. No one can really predict accurately what will happen to the emerging Blockchain Technology industry and market, but it is clear that there will be increased pressure on Tax compliance, and there are great opportunities for legal investments in cryptocurrency as its popularity and adoption are growing exponentially with time. It appears that Bitcoin and Blockchain technology are here to stay and grow stronger as Central Banks, Large Financial Institutions, and Global Assets Managers begin to accumulate them as reserves. As the new generation of millennials and Gen Z becomes a larger part of the financial markets, expect more adoption and use of digital assets and blockchain technologies products in their portfolios. Even if some cryptocurrencies fail, like FTX, and Terra

Classic, the mass adoption of the Bitcoin and Blockchain technology will continue.

Also, as an asset class, cryptocurrencies have unequivocally emerged as an asset class that cannot be ignored for their remarkable performance in the past decade and are now increasingly attracting institutional investors and global asset managers. The rise in the demand for Bitcoin and Bitcoin Technologies products requires a more professional assessment of the underlying sources of risks and opportunities. This calls for better risk management and techniques for the advancement of the market, which will include replacing self-regulation and automated governance with effective supervisory and regulatory structures. Whether Bitcoin and Blockchain Technologies currency will replace fiat money to some limited extent or not remains to be seen. But one thing is certain, the road toward a digital currency requires a clear, comprehensive, and global set of standards as it will continue to grow despite the lack of standard regulations. As a result of the meteoric rise of Bitcoin and other cryptocurrencies like Ethereum, Ripple, Solana, and Binance coin, and an increasing number of businesses, organizations, and corporate bodies accepting them as payment modes. Bitcoin and Blockchain technology tokens have become a readily emerging currency that the world should keep its eyes on.

CHAPTER 10

WHAT BITCOIN IS NOT?

Cryptocurrencies are many things to many people. To some, they are just fads; to some, they are a bubble; for some they are get rich quick, money doubling, Ponzi schemes, an instrument for fraud and money laundering for some, but Bitcoin and true Blockchain technology products are not for any of these. According to the wise words of the late Bahamian Business consultant Dr. Myles Munroe, "When the purpose of a thing is not known, abuse is inevitable." There is a lot of abuse in the Blockchain Industry and crypto space, which may be largely due to the lack of right, sound, and good understanding of what Bitcoin and Blockchain Technology are really all about. The understanding of the very idea, purpose, motives, and vision behind the creation of Bitcoin and Blockchain Technology by Satoshi Nakamoto will help us all to understand what our focus, energy, and motives should be when we are acting as players or users in the crypto space and blockchain industry.

It's a true saying that we do not see the world or things as they are, but as we are, as humans, our perceptions and perspectives determine how we approach and relate to things. As of today, we have over 22,000 known cryptocurrencies in the world today according to Forbes.[130] The question is, what is the motive, purpose, and problem that these digital coins and blockchain technology companies are trying to solve in the world? The crypto space has some dubious, fraudulent people who lack integrity and moral, and ethical standards, who are not about building real-world user cases, with a passion for solving socio-economic problems of nations, and revolutionizing the world's data management and value transfer methods, tackle financial challenges, poverty and lack that many people are faced with in the world.

Some cryptos are used as investment vehicles, others buy them as a store of value, while some use them for transactional purposes; developers in the blockchain industry have the rare privilege of building multi-diverse transactional tools, services, and communities using the blockchain technology. Michael Saylor, the renowned CEO of Business Intelligence firm Micro-Strategy, defined Bitcoin as a bank in cyberspace, run by incorruptible software, offering a global, affordable, simple, and secure savings account to billions of people who don't have the option or desire to run their own hedge funds. But He didn't see Bitcoin like this before; in 2013, he called it an online gambling that will soon come to its end,[131,] but a new perspective and paradigm make the difference. Now, he is a great business executive leader championing a great cause for Bitcoin and its lightning technology all over the world.

Bitcoin and Blockchain technology represent an important technological, financial, economic, and computer science innovation, and as such, a strong focus and energy should be directed towards these areas to provide lasting, impactful, valuable solutions to people and not to steal from them or destroy the nation's economy by misappropriating funds, going bankrupt.

Buying Bitcoin is analogous to buying tangible assets like gold real estate in cyberspace, and Bitcoin itself is an installation of the principle of conservation of energy in cyberspace; this escape is analogous to escaping Earth's gravity well to move in space, without gravity or atmospheric drag. Bitcoin is the first fair, shared, immutable, permissionless ledger that humans have ever had. From a moral, ethical point of view, it represents an ideology: a permissionless property rights for the over 8 billion people in the world. Bitcoin is an innovation that represents a digital commodity as opposed to a digital security that has an issuer. The Bitcoin mining network converts electricity to digital energy so that it is secure and impregnable for the long foreseeable future. Bitcoin's digital energy can be moved at the speed of light, friction-free, on a computer, across $10 billion computers, at high frequency, thousands of times a second. To accomplish this, you have to have a final settlement that is separate from a credit system or a security itself.

Bitcoin is an instrument of economic empowerment; a bitcoin purchased in Nigeria is exactly the same bitcoin purchased in Manhattan. Crypto digital commodities like Bitcoin are innovative, and several Crypto exchanges that trade 24/7, 365 days in a year, are a novelty for the investing public. Bitcoin and cryptos are US dollar proxies running on crypto rails. The market cap of these digital assets will keep growing because as many people buy into them as an escape from the rapid inflation and devaluation of local currencies. It is important to know that Bitcoin is a digital energy, a digital commodity that is capped at 21 million units, decentralized, running on millions of servers, and supported by hundreds of millions of people all around the world. Nobody can change it. It represents the first fair, shared, immutable ledger humans have ever had and represents the singularity where we finally put energy, money, property, or matter into cyberspace.

Imagine what can be done easily with a billion dollars of Bitcoin. You can move it between a million computers every second for free, and you can program it, but there is no way to do a million final settlement transactions on a computer network using credit, using a credit card, using a bank, using a fiat currency. Technically, Bitcoin represents the digital transformation of energy. In the next 20 to 30 years there will be a transformation of energy into cyberspace. One of the reasons why Bitcoin has value is because it's backed by a $20 billion dollar network of bitcoin miners that are taking electricity and they are running it through a SHA-256 protocol in order to hast it. And that $20 billion worth of electricity every four years is like $5 billion of electricity a year, and that $20 billion hardware that represents the network that decentralizes Bitcoin, secures it, keeps anyone from being able to hack it, and makes it impossible to any kind or cheat, manipulation, theft, or threat. Bitcoin innovation is the creation of a digital commodity as opposed to digital security, its very easy to put a coupon, or a security, on a database. The 100,000 coupons and the 100,000 securities will all ultimately require a bank, a company, and a government in order to run them.

If you wanted to have in your possession something that is scarce and desirable for the next 100 years, and you don't trust the CEO, you don't trust the company, you don't trust the bank, you don't trust the government, and you don't trust the state, and you want to transcend all these things, then you will need something like Bitcoin's network that doesn't use software. That's why Bitcoin runs on proof-of-work, and it converts the electricity into a block of digital energy, which is secure, potentially for the next 1,000 years. This is very important because when corporations, governments, institutional investors, and high net-worth individuals who want to move billions of dollars of money in hundreds of millions of transactions, at the speed of light, friction-free, on computers, across $10 billion computers, at high frequency, like 40 times a second, or 40,000 times a second, you have to have a final settlement that is apart from a credit system or security itself.

The energy embedded in things is what makes them a commodity. If we take energy out of an apple, or out of steel, or out of a building, or out of soybean, it won't be a commodity anymore, but rather a security, a coupon. If we take the electricity in Bitcoin out of it and use software, we will need to create a software company issuing coupons that circulate around a network. And the best case is it's going to be security that will be regulated by the SEC, because the software engineers can control whether or not you get to use it. The worst case is that it will be just a coupon, so the electricity in the Bitcoin network is the price it pays for us to have a commodity, and a commodity is critical if we want a neutral, international, open monetary system, global money that is permissionless and neutral.

Having bitcoin and keeping or holding it as an asset requires that we have a long-term perspective, of an average of 10 years as a hedge against depreciating fiat currency inflation as against buying for quick get rich fast means. Sooner or later, Bitcoin will replace or compete with Gold as a non-sovereign store of value asset. Gold is a $10 trillion asset right now, and Bitcoin is digital gold, and it is 100 times better than Gold. You can't inflate it, that half-life of money in Bitcoin is forever, you can move it on billions of computers at the speed of light. Based on predictions, if Bitcoin goes to the value of Gold, it's going to be valued at $500,000 per unit Bitcoin, and they believe this can happen within 10-15 years as more mainstream institutional investors and corporations' adoption increases rapidly.

With time, when Bitcoin becomes a trillion-dollar asset in the crypto world and eventually becomes a $10 trillion dollar replacement for gold as a precious metal, people will begin to see it as a superior property to real estate or any physical property because you can't move a billion-dollar building from New York to San Francisco, but you can move a billion-dollar block of Bitcoin from New York to San Francisco. Bitcoin represents

Crypto Property, and if you live in Africa, like Nigeria, for example, and I give you $50,000, there is nothing you would want to buy anywhere in Nigeria for $50,000 that represents a superior property to buying $50,000 worth of Bitcoin.

Not even barrels of crude oil, which many of the political leaders would fight themselves, or natural mineral resources that they would even almost kill for, is superior to Bitcoin because one Bitcoin valued at almost $27,000 today is worth 300 barrels of crude oil, which is a staggering 47,000 liters of Crude oil.[132] Bitcoin is an instrument for economic empowerment and financial freedom. Bitcoin can serve as a way to give property rights to everybody with a $40 Android phone anywhere on earth by giving them something they can own that can't be debased or devalued, that they can carry anywhere with them for the rest of their life. Bitcoin property rights give them Pari-passu rights. For example, again, if you live in Nigeria and you own a $200,000 real estate property, it's not the same as a $200,000 real estate property in New York, but the value of the same $200,000 Bitcoin that you have in Nigeria is same with what you have in New York, and you have the same economic rights and financial power in both locations, anywhere in the world with Bitcoin.

I believe strongly that in the long run, a few decades from now, Bitcoin will be viewed by most people in the world as a long-term store of value, their savings account to hedge against inflation, devaluation, and economic crisis. We already have ideas about mobile apps that will be a killer app or viral apps that are built on Android or iPhones that support lightning, that hold Bitcoin for long-term savings accounts, and hold USD or any other fiat currency as a short-term, immediate medium of exchange. Once we start having Blockchain technology products like this and it's been launched out there for real-world use, it's going to spread to millions of people, then billions of people, and yes, they will use it every day for their daily life, economic and financial activities. Fiat currencies like Dollar, Naira, and Pounds most likely won't go away. What's going to go away is the weakest hundred local currencies. People will dump the failing local currencies for stronger currencies like the dollar. Bitcoin will be used as a long-term store of value for people who want to protect their money, wealth and transfer their generational wealth and legacy to their children.

CHAPTER 11

THE FUTURE OF MONEY & EMERGING TECHNOLOGIES

W ho knows what the future really holds? You will probably have heard many people that say, "Nobody, that only God knows what the future holds." But like the wise words of the 16th President of America, Abraham Lincoln says, "The Best way to predict the future is to create it." We can know what the future holds in store for us as we observe how we have evolved, developed, transformed, and grown as humans over the years, decades, centuries, and millenniums. Our recognition and representation of what is value and what money is, have transformed and taken on different turns and dynamics with the advancement of newer, better, faster, and more efficient technologies that we are creating as humans every day.

At the beginning of this book, we talked about the history of money and finance. As we draw closer to the final pages of this book, we will be looking at the projections and forecast of what the future of money, finance, economy, and lifestyle holds in store for us as people, with the various emerging technologies that are helping to make our world and lives a better one and more efficient one. Emerging Technologies are a wide range of technologies whose development, practical applications, or both are still largely unrealized, that are set to revolutionize major human affairs such as educational technology, information technology, nanotechnology, biotechnology, robotics, artificial intelligence, internet of things, and blockchain technology which we've talked about extensively in various pages across this book.

Distributed ledger that provides a transparent and immutable list of transactions, with a wide range of uses as an open, decentralized database required ranging from logistics & supply chains to cryptocurrencies, was first conceived by Nick Szabo in 1994 but remained unrealized until the development of Blockchain by Satoshi Nakamoto in 2009. Smart contracts have further been developed as self-executing transactions which occur when pre-defined conditions are met, with the aim of providing security that is superior to traditional contract law and to reduce transaction costs and delays.

Once upon a time, gold and silver coins were used as a medium of exchange and seen as money at one time in history, although today, gold has metamorphosed into a store of value. If we are to move $1 billion gold coins from Tokyo to the USA today, it will take us about 3 months and cost $5 million dollars to do that. If we are to move the same amount of $1 billion dollars from Tokyo to Canada, using our modern-day cross-border payment systems, it will take like 2-3 days and a cost fee of 0.2% at least and 4.3% of the most expensive payment providers offering international money transfer services.[133] 0.2% of $1 Billion dollars is a staggering $20 million dollars, whereas with Bitcoin and Blockchain technology today, we can move the same $1 billion dollars within minutes with a fee charge that sounds so unimaginably true, but it is so true and real, at a cost fee of $5.[134] The Bitcoin Network and newly developed Blockchain technology products are well known for their very low transaction fees, and fast cross-border, international payments systems without the involvement of a third-party. This is currently changing the dynamics of the world's global financial systems, and many business tycoons, moguls, and Fortune 500 CEOs are now looking into the various ways and methods they can use to leverage this new blockchain technology for the financial world.

It has been said by many that the future of money and value transfer all around the world in the coming decades will be dominated by blockchain technologies. Even the world's international monetary governing bodies, like IMF, World Economic Forum, and World Bank, have also backed up this claim in their conferences and publications. We humans, by nature, are ordinarily and primarily driven by better technology, ease, comfort, efficiency, convenience, and reliability of emerging technologies and new ways of doing things that help to better and make our lives easier.

Just as there is still use of gold, silver, and other precious commodities as means of value transfer in the world today, despite the use of our fiat paper currencies and electronic payments systems, the advent of bitcoin and blockchain technology will not totally take out or replace the fiat paper currency of your country, they will still most likely be in used but not dominantly. Bitcoin and Blockchain technology products will be the major players and focus of most financial institutions and asset managers for stores of value and wealth transfer all across the globe. The world today is changing at a very fast, dynamic speed, and only the people who can learn and unlearn, and relearn and learn again repeatedly will be able to gain a competitive advantage over those who don't learn and adapt to new emerging technologies in their world.

For example, we all saw how the emergence of the Internet made it possible for news, articles, and magazines to be read online by many people all at the same time at a fast rate on blogs and social media news houses, thereby putting a lot of media printing press houses out of business. The same goes for the big major supermarkets and supply chains like Walmart that we once had, which are now losing their competition to the new world-leading e-commerce firm Amazon. The same thing can be seen in the home-made movies and cinema industries with the emergence of entertainment platforms like Netflix, as many of the big media entertainment industries lost their advantage. We can even further see this with the emergence of Uber, Lyft in the transportation industry and Air BnB in the hospitality and housing industry.

It is, therefore, of utmost importance that we prepare ourselves for the emerging changes coming to the financial industry and economy of the world. This would probably most likely have the most impact as finance is involved, and like we said earlier, money, finance, and the economy affects everyone. We must ensure that we are well positioned ahead of our times and contemporaries to be able to take advantage of competitive opportunities and privileges before they are widely accepted and endorsed by the popular, mainstream people.

Emerging technologies like Artificial Intelligence Robotics, Internet of Things, Modern Science, IVFs, and many others out there in the world are already helping millions of people to solve their major problems and challenges that they could not have probably imagined solving by themselves without the advent of these technologies. In the same vein, a lot of financial problems and economic challenges in the world today are being tackled and solved with blockchain technologies.

As we approach a more cashless future, we are already seeing the use of credit card and mobile phone payments disrupting the use of the physical cash market, but the major real driving force will still most likely be the mainstream adoption of institutional investors and central banks, as new cryptocurrencies and blockchain technology continue to emerge and their awareness expands. The far-reaching implications of this revolution for individuals, businesses, banks, and governments which include improved monetary efficiency, increased flexibility, and improved financial access, especially for the unbanked, as everything from consumer banking to monetary policy and international payments is being revolutionized by these new emerging technologies.

As of today, Bitcoin and other blockchain coins like Ethereum, Ripple, etc., may not be used as a medium of exchange for day-to-day transactions like the dollar fiat currency due to their high volatility nature; they are more suitable as stores of value. Day-to-day transactions for basic things like groceries, books, etc., are being carried out with digital payment systems and technologies that are at very low cost. There are many people in several countries who don't have access to digital payments, they don't have access to basic banking products and services. Payment systems providers are currently dominating the payment systems with better innovations, fast transactions, and low cost or fee charges as compared to commercial Banks, and the banks are beginning to feel threatened by their competition.

The competition for the future of money is bound between two ends, one end driven by the continued desire of central banks and governments to centralize, issue, and control the fiat paper currency system and its emerging digital versions like the CBDCs and the other end being to permit the decentralized and independent private limited supply of money facilitated by emerging technologies such as Blockchain, as in the case of Bitcoin and Cryptocurrencies. These competitions and dynamics are further reflected and escalated by the regulatory state of the two ends.

The regulatory framework for the issuance and use of fiat money has been consistent with security improvements and durability noted with stable banknotes and widespread use as compared to the regulatory framework of Bitcoin and Cryptocurrencies that are widely unregulated and dominated by bans and outright restrictions in some countries despite the wild growing interest in digital currencies all over the world. But these dynamics are changing as the digital currencies are evolving and gaining mainstream adoption, and regulatory changes and adoption are taking place with time, in a few decades from now.

We can boldly look ahead and predict ahead that the three main historical functions of money are as a unit of currency, the medium of exchange, and store of value will not change. This is the only certainty that we know about the future of money. A lot of change and revolution is already taking place in many countries all over the world as governments and policy-makers are now shifting to a cashless society with the aim of displacing cash for many factors, economic and social reasons through a cashless infrastructure and electronic payment systems that facilitate financial services in all sectors of the economy and provides secure, reliable and user-centric financial solutions in compliance with international standards is now taking center stage. It is strongly believed that the use of cryptocurrencies and digital payments will help to reduce the use of cash for illicit and fraudulent transactions like terrorism, drug trafficking, money laundering, bribery, weapon sales, etc. and, create an efficient monetary system, and save cost for governments.

To maintain their sovereign control over the issuance and use of money, Central Banks across the world are concentrating their efforts on defining, regulating, or outrightly banning and building stronger oversight over new forms of money being pursued by private individuals and institutional assets managers as ways of democratizing the central banks control over the issuance and use of money.

It is evidently true that the world we know it as today has changed tremendously in the last four years, as we have witnessed huge changes to our ways of work and life than we experienced some decades ago, which is largely due to the advances in emerging technologies, global responses to global challenges such as the Covid-19 pandemic, and the surge in entrepreneurial pursuits resulting in new Startups leveraging on the opportunities of these emerging technologies to address existing and new customers pain points. The results have been seen largely in the digitalization of almost all known human activities, from our physical, and social meetings and boardroom meetings to virtual Zoom and Microsoft teams meetings. Also, in the areas of finance and money, as Dan Schulman, the CEO of PayPal, has rightly said, "Physical money, whether in the form of a cheque, cash or credit card, it's digitizing that is in front of us."

Globally, digital transaction value grew by 22% between 2021 and 20222 from $1 trillion dollar to around $1.26 trillion, while the share of cash-based transactions in the overall transactions declined by 2% due to the significant rise in digital transactions. We should expect more of this in the coming years and decades ahead and prepare ourselves very well for the economic and financial changes coming ahead as their growth will be driven by emerging technologies like Contactless Cards, AI Robotics, Internet of Things, QR Codes, Voice Initiated Payment services like Alexa, Siri, Google Assistant amongst many other emerging technological developments.

CHAPTER 12
THE LEVEL PLAYING FIELD IS NOW YOURS... WILL YOU PLAY? OR YOU'LL STAY ON THE SIDELINES?

The World's global financial system has always seemed to be a rigged system with a covert playbook that only a few elites, ultra HNI individuals, wealthy families, institutions, and governments had access to in their favor and advantage, which serves them only and leave the general populace of people all over the world in loss, economic troubles, financial constraints, and lack. Money, Finance, and Economy are things that affect everybody in the world, as our daily living, survival, and activities depend on the world's global financial system.

We lose our money and wealth that we toiled hard and labored diligently for to inflation, national currency devaluation, economic depression, recession, geopolitical wars, global economic crisis, corruption, government misappropriations of funds, wrong economic policies and regulations set by our political leaders and policymakers that keeps us working and working even into our retirement age, with barely little or nothing to hold on to with value.

But now this narrative and dynamics is changing now, with the innovation and creation of Bitcoin and Blockchain technology. The very idea was born out of the global economic financial crisis that happened in 2008-2009, which left many people losing their money, wealth, and assets to economic forces with powers beyond their control. The advent of Bitcoin and Blockchain technology over the last decade is now changing the world's global financial system and leveling the playing field for everyone to take advantage of it for their financial freedom while also hedging their money, wealth, and assets against all national and global economic forces that they cannot fight against or beat.

Many individuals are now setting the pace and blazing the trails for others to follow as they champion the cause for financial freedom, financial independence, productivity, economic growth, and national development in their various fields, especially in the Blockchain industry. We are privileged and greatly blessed to have been born at a time such as this, where we can determine our own financial future by ourselves and make a lasting, valuable impact in the lives of our family, friends, community, society, countries, and the world at large. Many a generation would have loved to have this great opportunity and advantage that we have access to now with Bitcoin and Blockchain Technology which they did not have access to in their own days and time.

The very idea of you working for 30 to 35 years to your retirement and saving our fiat money currency in banks, and yet we grow old to discover the shocking reality of our lives that all that we toiled and labored for, for decades with our youthful years and energy are worth barely anything and we can't live off the money for the rest of our lives. Our invested stocks, mutual funds, and 401k funds have been severely battered by economic forces of national debts, inflation, currency devaluation, economic recession, depression, geopolitical wars, bad governments, and corrupt officials and policymakers.

Once upon a time, building a thriving business and industrial company took a huge amount and expensive capital to set up, which many of us today cannot even afford, with all the risks and challenges involved in building a viable business that will help to create jobs for many people and help us achieve financial freedom. Many of us are not from ultra-wealthy homes, palatial houses, and royal families where we have all that we would ever need for our present lives and future ready made and prepared for us by our wealthy parents. We've mostly had to compete for quality education, strive to get good jobs with good incomes to cater to our immediate and family needs, put out our best efforts to be self-reliant and productive, to create value, and create success for ourselves.

The odds of surviving, thriving, and achieving financial independence and economic freedom are really hard for the average ordinary individual who has no strong background, especially in the developing countries in Asia and Africa. But the advent of Bitcoin and Blockchain technology, like every other technology like (Internet, Modern Science), has come to provide a level playing field in the financial sector for everyone to take advantage of. We can now control and self-custody our own money and wealth without involving any third central party like Banks or Governments. What a privilege and great opportunity this is for us. We can now build valuable solutions and blockchain products that help to solve real-world problems that provide freedom for people. What a privilege and great opportunity this is for us. We can now grow our wealth and build good legacies with our families as we experience the joy of financial independence and freedom. What a privilege and opportunity this is for us.

But it's not enough to have all these opportunities and privileges before us, and we are not deploying them, taking advantage of them, building our families and societies on the solid foundation of integrity, truth, justice, mercy, and welfare for all. Many people will still choose to be on the sidelines without taking the actions needed to learn, prepare, and equip themselves with the knowledge and skills needed to utilize and take advantage of the Bitcoin and Blockchain technology for their personal growth, development, and societal economic advancement. As we can see in the previous chapters of this book, many people are already taking the right steps and actions needed to build and achieve financial freedom and a good legacy for themselves by using Bitcoin and Blockchain technology.

Nothing good in life comes easy, and nothing that is of worthwhile value is without its fair price. Financial freedom and independence have its fair price, and the real question is are you willing to pay the price for it? Even though the innovation of Bitcoin and Blockchain Technology has helped to make the method of payment easy. But the price of learning, education, diligence, value creation, courage, taking calculated risks, networking, building quality relationships, helping the needy and caring for people genuinely, persistence, patience, and constant improvement will still need to be paid.

I really hope that you've been inspired, enlightened, encouraged, and educated through your journey of reading this book and that great value has been added to your personality and person. As we come towards the end of this book, I would like you to know that information or knowledge known is not enough, as it is not only information or knowledge that changes our lives, but the actions and decisions that we take and make on the basis of the information and knowledge that we've gained that really transforms and revolutionize our lives, and helps us to achieve our financial goals, family goals, community goals, and national goals.

Recently, we've seen how people living in and citizens of countries like Turkey, Argentina, Zimbabwe, Nigeria, and several other countries all around the world are facing hard, tough economic challenges because of the tough economic hardship that is making millions of them to lose their money to hyper-inflation, double-digit interest rates, the rapid devaluation of their currencies, economic recession and depression that has left a lot of families in turmoil, discomfort, and financial hardship. I believe that through the knowledge and information shared in this book, we would be able to protect ourselves, our families, our loved ones, and our communities from these national and global economic forces that are stronger than us and, bad governments, corrupt banks, and wrong economic policies.

The world's global economic and financial system field, which was not evenly leveled for thousands of years, has now been evenly leveled by Bitcoin and Blockchain Technologies, but the real question is, will you take the right actions and decisions to develop and equip yourself and play in the leveled field to achieve financial independence and freedom or you will still remain on the sidelines and be fighting hard to stay above the high waters of financial crisis, turmoil, and decadence. Just as it is with Bitcoin, the sovereign choice is Yours! to decide.

BIBLIOGRAPHY

1. Colossians 1:16-17
2. Glyn Davies. "A History of Money" chapter 2. University of Wales Press Cardiff, 2016.
3. Cambridge University. "Radiocarbon-Dating an Early minting site: the emergence of Standardized Coinage in China."
4. World History Encyclopedia. "The Invention of the First Coinage in Ancient Lydia". Britannica. "Origin of Coins"
5. Hans Ulrich Vogel. "Macro Polo was in China: New Evidence from Currencies, Salts, and Revenues." Page 94. BRILL, 2012
6. Britannica. "Coinage In Western Continental Europe, Africa, and The Byzantine Empire"
7. Coinmarketcap. "Bitcoin marketcap"
8. Bitcoin Price History Chart. https://buybitcoinworldwide.com/price/#:
9. Coinmarketcap. "Bitcoin marketcap"
10. Forbes. "Forbes.com/advisor/investing/cryptocurrency/different-types-of-cryptocurrencies/"
11. Forbes. "Forbes.com/advisor/investing/cryptocurrency/different-types-of-cryptocurrencies/"
12. WiseVoter. https://wisevoter.com/country-rankings/inflation-by-country/
13. WiseVoter. https://wisevoter.com/country-rankings/inflation-by-country/
14. Forbes.com https://www.forbes.com/sites/hanktucker/2023/04/04/the-richest-hedge-fund-managers-2023/?sh=565e91b05713
15. Daniel 5:12
16. PWC. "Global Economy Watch – Projections > Real GDP/Inflation > Share of 2016 world GDP".
17. Treasury.Gov "Debt to the penny"
18. The New York Times. https://www.nytimes.com/2008/10/03/business/worldbusiness/03iht-bailout.4.16679355.html
19. Corporate Finance Institute Resources. https://corporatefinanceinstitute.com/resources/capital-markets/lehman-brothers/
20. BBC. bbc.com/news/business-45243088 "Greece emerges from Eurozone bailout program"

21. Adam Tooze, The Wages of Destruction: The Making and Breaking of the Nazi Economy (2008)

22. Yahoo Finance. https://finance.yahoo.com/news/us-dollar-value-plummeting-does-162347145.

23. Britanica. https://www.britannica.com/event/hyperinflation-in-the-Weimar-Republic

24. Bitcoin.org "Bitcoin: A Peer-to-Peer Electronic Cash System"

25. Bitcoin.org "Bitcoin: A Peer-to-Peer Electronic Cash System"

26. Coinmarketcap.com report 5th September 2023

27. BBC. https://www.bbc.com/news/business-64245044 "FTX: Collapsed crypto giant recovers over $5bn of assets"

28. BBC. https://www.bbc.com/news/business-64245044 "FTX: Collapsed crypto giant recovers over $5bn of assets"

29. BBC. https://www.bbc.com/news/business-64245044 "FTX: Collapsed crypto giant recovers over $5bn of assets"

30. Bloomberg.com https://www.bloomberg.com/news/articles/2022-06-23/kwon-tells-wsj-he-lost-nearly-all-his-wealth-after-terra-crash. "Terra co-founder lost nearly all His wealth in wipeout, WSJ says"

31. The New York Times https://www.nytimes.com/2022/05/18/technology/terra-luna-cryptocurrency-do-kwon.html

32. CoinDesk https://www.coindesk.com/layer2/2022/06/28/secs-gensler-reiterates-bitcoin-alone-is-a-commodity-is-he-right/

33. Binance.com https://www.binance.com/en-NG/feed/post/606605 "Breaking: SEC sues Coinbase after Binance, lists 13 tokens as Security."

34. Coinmarketcap.com https://coinmarketcap.com/legal-tender-countries/

35. Coinmarketcap.com Bitcoin (BTC) report 5th September 2023

36. Coinmarketcap.com Ethereum (ETH) report 5th September 2023

37. Forbes. *"The Richest People In Cryptocurrency". Forbes. 6 February 2018. Archived from the original on 2018-02-26.*

38. CompaniesMarketCap. https://companiesmarketcap.com/meta-platforms/marketcap/

39. The Guardian. https://www.theguardian.com/technology/2009/feb/12/facebook-mark-zuckerberg-ex-classmates

40. The Washington Post. https://www.washingtonpost.com/news/the-switch/wp/2013/11/09/the-11-million-in-bitcoins-the-winklevoss-brothers-bought-is-now-worth-32-million/

41. The Washington Post. https://www.washingtonpost.com/news/the-switch/wp/2013/11/09/the-11-million-in-bitcoins-the-winklevoss-brothers-bought-is-now-worth-32-million/

42. Binance News. https://www.binance.com/en/feed/post/1065459 "SEC's first deadlines to approve 7 Bitcoin ETFs"

43. Forbes. https://www.forbes.com/profile/tyler-winklevoss/?sh= 4d51259e2cbd

44. Forbes. https://www.forbes.com/profile/tyler-winklevoss/?sh= 4d51259e2cbd

45. Forbes. "Forbes Rich List 2020: The 5 Youngest Billionaires in Asia". *Tatler Hong Kong*. 15 May 2020.

46. Browne, Ryan (2022-07-18). "Crypto exchange Binance fined $3.4 million by Dutch central bank for operating illegally". *CNBC*.

47. "Bloomberg Billionaires Index: Changpeng Zhao". *Bloomberg.com*. Bloomberg L.P. Archived from the original on 2022-01-12

48. "Patents by Inventor Michel J Saylor." Justia.com 13 May 2016.

49. Forbes. "MicroStrategy adds to its Bitcoin stash in Q2, crypto aids results."

50. Forbes. "MicroStrategy adds to its Bitcoin stash in Q2, crypto aids results."

51. Andrews, Edmund L. (September 24, 2013). "Chris Larsen: Money Without Borders". Stanford Graduate School of Business.

52. Coinmarketcap.com Ripple (XRP) report 7th September 2023

53. Popper, Nathaniel (January 4, 2018). *"Rise of Bitcoin Competitor Ripple Creates Wealth to Rival Zuckerberg"*. *The New York Times*.

54. Forbes. "Chris Larsen's profile" https://www.forbes.com/profile/ chris-larsen/?sh=571fdf2957ed

55. Forbes. "Tim Draper's profile" https://www.forbes.com/profile/ tim-draper/?sh=63eaf407af34

56. Coinmarketcap.com Bitcoin (BTC) report 7th September 2023

57. CoinDesk. https://www.coindesk.com/business/2023/07/11/tim-draper-still-thinks-bitcoin-can-reach-250k-just-2-years-later-than-he-expected/

58. Crunchbase. https://www.crunchbase.com/organization/galaxy-interactive/investor_financials

59. Bloomberg. "A Crypto Fund King Says Bitcoin Will Be the Biggest Bubble Ever". Bloomberg. 26 September 2017.

60. Lee, Isabelle (May 14, 2021). "Billionaire Mike Novogratz reveals that crypto makes up 85% of his wealth — and says ether can surge another 23%". Business Insider.

61. "'Billions' Recap, Season 5, Episode 8: Back in Business". The New York Times.

62. RogerVer. "Biography, https://www.rogerver.com/bio/"

63. RogerVer "Biography, https://www.rogerver.com/bio/"

64. Forbes. https://www.forbes.com/sites/sergeiklebnikov/2022/10/14/legendary-value-investor-bill-miller-says-buy-bitcoin-and-8-other-stock-bargains/?sh=5f8ccc16a5b5

65. CoinDesk. coindesk.com/business/2022/01/10/billionaire-investor-bill-miller-now-has-50-of-his-personal-wealth-in-bitcoin/

66. CoinDesk. coindesk.com/business/2022/01/10/billionaire-investor-bill-miller-now-has-50-of-his-personal-wealth-in-bitcoin/

67. SMC DAO https://www.smcdao.com/

68. SMC DAO https://www.smcdao.com/

69. CNBC. https://www.cnbc.com/2021/07/06/millennial-dogecoin-millionaire-on-being-paid-in-dogecoin.html

70. Forbes. https://www.forbes.com/profile/elon-musk/?sh=9ad2d9f7999b

71. Forbes. https://www.forbes.com/sites/digital-assets/2023/04/03/a-legitimate-cryptocurrency-dogecoin-price-suddenly-soars-after-elon-musk-hits-back-at-258-billion-lawsuit/?sh=59bd44424ba0

72. CNN. https://edition.cnn.com/2021/05/14/investing/crypto-shiba-inu-brothers-millionaires/index.html

73. CNN. https://edition.cnn.com/2021/05/14/investing/crypto-shiba-inu-brothers-millionaires/index.html

74. CNN. https://edition.cnn.com/2021/05/14/investing/crypto-shiba-inu-brothers-millionaires/index.html

75. Analytical Insight. https://www.analyticsinsight.net/how-to-make-millions-with-solana-sol-pancakeswap-cake-and-chronoly-crno/

76. Analytical Insight. https://www.analyticsinsight.net/how-to-make-millions-with-solana-sol-pancakeswap-cake-and-chronoly-crno/

77. Coingape. https://coingape.com/heres-how-much-your-100-investment-in-binance-coin-will-be-worth-if-bnb-reaches-500/

78. Outlook. https://www.outlookindia.com/business-spotlight/wld-reaches-20-billion-market-cap-straight-after-launch-can-worldcoin-be-the-next-bitcoin-news-306092

79. Forbes. https://www.forbes.com/advisor/au/investing/cryptocurrency/what-is-worldcoin/

80. Worldometers. https://www.worldometers.info/world-population/

81. Forbes. https://www.forbes.com/billionaires/

82. Global Citizen. https://www.globalcitizen.org/en/content/wealth-inequality-oxfam-billionaires-elon-musk/

83. Global Citizen. https://www.globalcitizen.org/en/content/wealth-inequality-oxfam-billionaires-elon-musk/

84. Global Citizen. https://www.globalcitizen.org/en/content/wealth-inequality-oxfam-billionaires-elon-musk/

85. Global Citizen. https://www.globalcitizen.org/en/content/wealth-inequality-oxfam-billionaires-elon-musk/

86. Global Citizen. https://www.globalcitizen.org/en/content/wealth-inequality-oxfam-billionaires-elon-musk/

87. Global Citizen. https://www.globalcitizen.org/en/content/wealth-inequality-oxfam-billionaires-elon-musk/

88. Isaiah 5:13 and Hosea 4:6

89. Proverbs 4:7-8

90. CBS News. https://www.cbsnews.com/news/financial-literacy-us-teens-compare/

91. Technext24 https://technext24.com/2023/03/06/bitcoin-a-legal-tender-el-salvadors/

92. IBM. "Basic Blockchain Security" https://www.ibm.com/topics/blockchain-security#:~:text=Each%20new%20block%20connects%20to,transaction%20is%20true%20and%20correct.

93. Finimize.com https://finimize.com/content/Q29udGVudFBpZWNlOjU3NzA=/bitcoin-security-heres-what-makes-the-og-blockchain-safer-than-fort-knox-with-ledger

94. CBS News. https://www.cnbc.com/2023/09/11/western-sanctions-on-russia-could-push-the-brics-alliance-closer-appec.html

95. The Economic Times. https://economictimes.indiatimes.com/news/international/business/russias-currency-hits-the-lowest-level-since-beginning-of-the-war-in-ukraine/articleshow/102725566.cms?from=mdr

96. CBS News. https://www.cbsnews.com/news/ruble-to-usd-less-than-a-penny-lowest-ukraine-war/

97. Forbes India. https://www.forbesindia.com/article/explainers/top-10-largest-economies-in-the-world/86159/1

98. The Global Economy. theglobaleconomy.com/rankings/gdp_share/

99. CEPR https://cepr.org/voxeu/columns/bystander-effect-us-china-trade-war#:~:text=The%20US%20imposed%20tariffs%20on,hikes%2C%20the%20existing%20ones%20remain.

100. https://carnegieendowment.org/2011/09/15/currency-wars-pub-45559#:~:text=In%20September%202010%2C%20Brazilian%20Finance,undervalued%20Chinese%20renminbi%20(RMB).

101. IG.com https://www.ig.com/en/news-and-trade-ideas/yuan-touches-11-year-low-190805

102. NBC News. https://www.nbcnews.com/news/investigations/china-helps-russia-evade-sanctions-tech-used-ukraine-war-rcna96693

103. U.S News https://www.usnews.com/news/best-countries/slideshows/a-timeline-of-the-russia-ukraine-conflict

104. The Guardian https://www.theguardian.com/business/2022/apr/19/russia-preparing-legal-action-to-unfreeze-600bn-foreign-currency-reserves

105. AL Jazeera https://www.aljazeera.com/features/2023/8/24/can-brics-dethrone-the-us-dollar-itll-be-an-uphill-climb-experts-say

106. https://www.linkedin.com/pulse/brics-considers-bitcoin-game-changer-replace-us-altaji-cdaa-/

107. Bitcoin Magazine. https://bitcoinmagazine.com/culture/brics-nations-drive-bitcoin-adoption

108. FX Street. https://www.fxstreet.com/cryptocurrencies/news/bitcoin-on-track-for-mass-adoption-as-it-grows-faster-than-the-internet-202102100825

109. https://coinmarketcap.com/ 11th September 2023

110. The Guardian. https://guardian.ng/business-services/new-platform-to-deepen-inclusion-among-nigerias-unbanked-underbanked/#:~:text=Nigeria%20is%20one%20of%20the,a%20tier%2Dthree%20bank%20account

111. Pymnts.com https://www.pymnts.com/cryptocurrency/2022/federal-reserve-powell-stablecoins-money-is-not-just-another-consumer-product/

112. CATO Institute. https://www.cato.org/study/risks-of-cbdcs#:~:text=Put%20simply%2C%20a%20CBDC%20would,to%20its%20threat%20to%20privacy.

113. CoinDesk. https://www.coindesk.com/policy/2023/07/17/ron-desantis-promises-to-ban-cbdcs-if-elected-president/

114. Smart Valor. https://smartvalor.com/sv/news/bitcoin-traditional-assets

115. Forbes. https://www.forbes.com/sites/cbovaird/2021/11/10/bitcoin-hits-latest-all-time-high-close-to-69000-as-multiple-factors-drive-gains/?sh=658a1b5f2ec9

116. Chain Debrief. https://chaindebrief.com/meet-bitcon-etf-applications/

117. Forbes. https://www.forbes.com/advisor/investing/cryptocurrency/spot-bitcoin-etf/

118. Coin Desk. https://www.coindesk.com/business/2023/07/14/blackrock-ceo-larry-fink-talks-up-crypto-demand-from-gold-investors/

119. Coin Desk. https://www.coindesk.com/business/2023/07/14/blackrock-ceo-larry-fink-talks-up-crypto-demand-from-gold-investors/

120. Coinmarketcap.com https://coinmarketcap.com/ Bitcoin (BTC) report 22nd September 2023

121. Coinmarketcap.com https://coinmarketcap.com/ Global Crypto Market Cap 22nd September 2023

122. CNBC https://www.cnbc.com/2022/07/14/why-the-2022-crypto-winter-is-unlike-previous-bear-markets.html

123. CNBC https://www.cnbc.com/2022/07/14/why-the-2022-crypto-winter-is-unlike-previous-bear-markets.html

124. Binance.com "The Biggest hack in crypto history, how they happened."

125. https://www.binance.com/en/feed/post/952859#:~:text=The%20largest%20cryptocurrency%20hack%20to,Ethereum%20and%20the%20USDC%20stablecoin.

126. Binance.com https://www.binance.com/en/feed/post/952859

127. Binance.com https://www.binance.com/en-NG/feed/post/1126767?ref=54670029

128. Investopedia. https://www.investopedia.com/terms/s/silk-road.asp

129. Money.com https://money.com/cryptocurrency-legal-status-by-country/

130. Forbes.com https://www.forbes.com/advisor/investing/cryptocurrency/

131. Cointelegraph.com https://cointelegraph.com/news/microstrategy-s-now-bullish-ceo-explains-why-he-bashed-bitcoin-back-in-2013

132. Countryeconomy.com https://countryeconomy.com/raw-materials/brent

133. Monito.com https://www.monito.com/send-money/japan/united-states/jpy/usd

134. Cointelegraphm.com https://cointelegraph.com/news/someone-transferred-a-billion-dollars-in-bitcoin-for-less-than-5

ABOUT THE AUTHOR

Leke Reddington is a global citizen with a coat of many colors that wears many hats. He is an astute Wealth Manager with experience gained while working with one of the world's biggest bank and largest bank in Africa, Standard Bank. He is the co-founder of Brainiac Strategy, a business intelligence firm with a focus in blockchain software development, cyber security, and digital assets management. He is the chief strategy officer of Africa's #1 largest digital Hedge Fund, Brainiac Capitalx. He travels the world to speak yearly at conferences, events, and seminars as a Kingdom Speaker. He functions in the role of a sagacious economist, political strategist, and special adviser to presidents and world leaders to proffer solutions on their nation's financial and socioeconomic problems and challenges. His reputation precedes him as a man with deep understanding, courage, integrity, and a strong passion for truth, justice, and good welfare for everyone. He is often called the Ray Dalio of Africa by his close friends and associates.